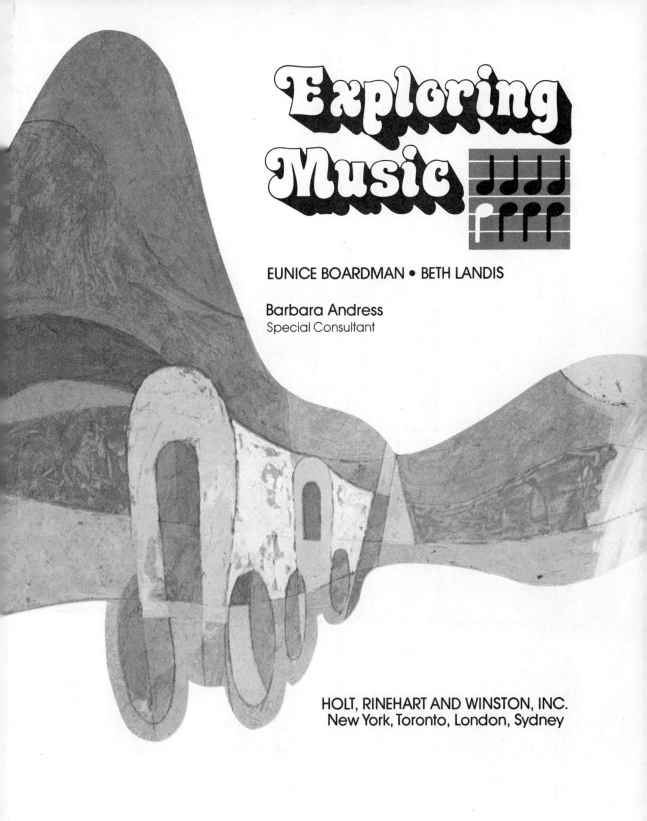

Exploring Music

EUNICE BOARDMAN • BETH LANDIS

Barbara Andress
Special Consultant

HOLT, RINEHART AND WINSTON, INC.
New York, Toronto, London, Sydney

Consultants

Milton Babbitt	Dorothy K. Gillett	Virginia Stroh Red
Keith E. Baird	Alan Lomax	Fela Sowande
Louis W. Ballard	Kurt Miller	Kurt Stone
Chou Wen-chung	Elena Paz	Nelmatilda Woodard

Music autography by Maxwell Weaner

Illustrated by Robert Shore
        Melanie G. Arwin
        Melanie Roher

Acknowledgments

Grateful acknowledgment is given to the following authors and publishers.

Behrman House, Inc. for "O Hanukah." Reprinted from *Gateway to Jewish Song* by Judith Eisenstein, published by Behrman House, Inc., 1261 Broadway, New York, N. Y. 10001. Used by permission.

Central Conference of American Rabbis for words to "Rock of Ages" by Frances Fox Sandmel *et al.*, from *Union Songster*, published by the Central Conference of American Rabbis. Used by permission.

Cooperative Recreation Service, Inc., for "Whippoorwill" by Anne H. Chapin from *Sing Together Children*, "Toembaï," from *101 Rounds*, "Take Time in Life," from *African Songs*, "Allelujah, Amen," from *Sacred Canons*, "Tina Singu," from *Songs To Keep*, and "Praise and Thanksgiving," from *Grace At Table*. Used by permission.

The John Day Company, Inc. for "Song of the Three 'Nots'" from *Folk Songs of China, Japan, Korea* by Betty Warner Dietz and Thomas Choonbai Park, copyright © 1964 by The John Day Company, Inc., publisher. Used by permission.

Gulf Music Company for the arrangement to "Song of the Sea," for the words to "Sweet Potatoes," and for "Farewell, My Own True Love," by William S. Haynie, copyright © 1966 by Gulf Music Company. Used by permission.

Harcourt Brace Jovanovich, Inc. for "The Farmer Is the Man," from *The American Songbag* by Carl Sandburg. Used by permission.

Trustees of the estate of Gustav Holst for the music to "In the Bleak Mid-Winter," used by permission of the Westminster Bank, Ltd., trustees of the estate of Gustav Holst.

Holt, Rinehart and Winston, Inc. for the poem "Dust of Snow" from *You Come Too* by Robert Frost, copyright 1923 by Holt, Rinehart and Winston, Inc., copyright 1951 by Robert Frost. Reprinted by permission of Holt, Rinehart and Winston, Inc.

Holt, Rinehart and Winston, Inc. for the poem "A Minor Bird" from *You Come Too* by Robert Frost, copyright 1928 by Holt, Rinehart and Winston, Inc., copyright © 1956 by Robert Frost. Reprinted by permission of Holt, Rinehart and Winston, Inc.

Lewis Music Publishing Company, Inc. for "Guantanamera," Spanish words by José Marti, English adaptation by Bernard Gasso, copyright © 1966 by Lewis Music Publishing Company, Inc. Used by permission.

Edward B. Marks Music Corporation for "Lift Every Voice and Sing," by J. Rosamund Johnson and James Weldon Johnson, copyright 1921 and later renewed by Edward B. Marks Music Corporation. Used by permission.

Contents

Let's Explore Music

Exploring music of the United States can be a fascinating and never-ending study. We are fortunate because so many kinds of music are available to us. Everyone can find music he will enjoy.

There is folk music of people from many nations who settled in the United States. Each group brought the music of its native land.

There are folk songs from our early history. As the pioneers worked to build the country, they sang songs that told of life in the new land.

There is folk music of today. People continue to create songs that speak of life as it is now — songs that help us express our own feelings and ideas.

Composed music of earlier times and different places is also important to us. American composers are influenced by the many styles and often combine these styles in their music. They seek to create music which is uniquely American as well.

Twentieth-century technology has helped us enjoy the many types of music. We can listen to music of all periods of history on recordings. We can hear and see famous performers on radio and television. We can attend concerts presented by artists from all over the world.

Explore the many musics that are part of American musical life. Compare the music of our own country with that of other lands. Discover the distinctive characteristics of the music of each region in the United States. Learn the skills which will help you perform the music you have discovered. Experiment with making music of your own.

This Land Is Your Land

Words and Music
by Woody Guthrie

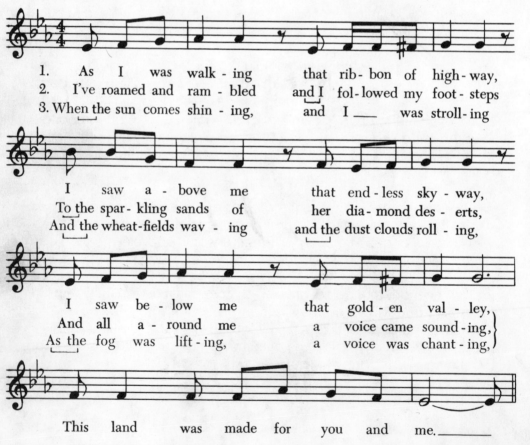

1. As I was walk - ing that rib - bon of high - way,
2. I've roamed and ram - bled and I fol - lowed my foot - steps
3. When the sun comes shin - ing, and I ___ was stroll - ing

I saw a - bove me that end - less sky - way,
To the spar - kling sands of her dia - mond des - erts,
And the wheat-fields wav - ing and the dust clouds roll - ing,

I saw be - low me that gold - en val - ley,
And all a - round me a voice came sound - ing,
As the fog was lift - ing, a voice was chant - ing,

This land was made for you and me. _____

2

Refrain

This land is your land, this land is my land,

From Cal - i - for - nia to the New York is - land,

From the red - wood for - est to the Gulf Stream wa - ters;

This land was made for you and me. _____

Springfield Mountain

American Folk Song

1. On Spring - field Moun - tain there did dwell
2. On Fri - day morn - ing he did go
3. When he re - ceived his death - ly wound,

A hand - some youth, was known full well,
Down to the mead - ows for to mow,
He laid his scythe up - on the ground,

Lieu - ten - ant Mer - rill's on - ly son,
He mowed, he mowed all round the field
For to re - turn was his in - tent,

A like - ly youth, full twen - ty - one.
With a poi - son-ous sar - pent at his heel.
Call - ing a - loud a-long as he went.

4. Day being past, night coming on,
   The father went to seek his son,
   And there he found his only son,
   Cold as a stone, dead on the ground.

5. He took him up and he carried him home,
   And on the way did weep and mourn,
   Saying, "I heard, but did not come,
   And now I'm left alone to mourn."

4

The Rattle Sna-wa-wake

American Folk Song

The ballad on the opposite page is the first song that we know originated in this country. Compare it with the version given below. What are the differences? Why do you think the changes occurred?

1. A   nice young ma - wa - wan Lived on   the   hi - wi - will;
2. He scarce had   mo - wo - wowed Half round the   fie - we - wield
3. "O   pap - py   da - wa - wad, Go   tell   my   ga - wa - wal

A   nice young ma - wa - wan, For I   knew him   we - we - well.
Come a rat-tle,come a sna - wa - wake And   bit him on the he - we - weel.
That I'm a-goin' to   di - wi - wie, For I   know I   sha - wa - wall."

Refrain

To   my   rat - tle,   to   my   roo - rah - ree.

4. "Oh John, O Joh-wa-wahn,
   Why did you go-wo-wo
   Way down in the mea-we-dow
   So far to mo-wo-wo?"
   Refrain

5. "Oh Sal, O Sa-wa-wa-wal,
   Why don't you kno-wo-wow
   When the grass gets ri-wi-wipe
   It must be mo-wo-wowed?"
   Refrain

6. Come all young gi-wi-wirls
   And shed a tea-we-wear
   For this young ma-wa-wan
   That died right he-we-were.
   Refrain

7. Come all young me-we-wen
   And warning ta-wa-wake
   And don't get bi-wi-wit
   By a rattle sna-wa-wake.
   Refrain

5

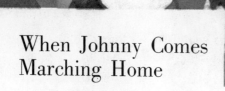

When Johnny Comes Marching Home

Words and Music
by Louis Lambert

1. When John - ny comes march-ing home a - gain, Hur - rah! ___ Hur-
2. The old ___ church bell will peal with joy, Hur - rah! ___ Hur-

rah! ___ We'll give him a heart - y wel - come then, Hur -
rah! ___ To wel - come home our dar - ling boy, Hur -

rah! ____ Hur - rah! ____ The _ men will cheer, _ the
rah! ____ Hur - rah! ____ The _ vil - lage lads ___ and

boys will shout, The la - dies, they _ will all turn out, }
lass - ies gay, With ros - es they _ will strew the way, } And we'll

all feel gay When John - ny comes march - ing home. ___

6

American Band Music

A ruffle of drums and blare of trumpets; the band is coming down the street! Who can hear that sound and not keep time with his feet?

Of all the sounds in music, there is probably no other that seems as truly American as the military band. In the late 1800's and early 1900's every community had its own band. There was a bandstand in the center of the park or village square where the band gave concerts on summer evenings. Some communities still carry on the tradition of summer band concerts.

Stars and Stripes Forever

by John Philip Sousa

Many composers have written marches for band, but John Philip Sousa is the most famous. He wrote more than a hundred marches, the best known of which is "Stars and Stripes Forever."

Listen to this march. Notice the design. There are two main sections. The first is called the **march** section. The second is the **trio**. As you listen to the music, determine the complete design. Listen for repetitions, changes in instrumentation, dynamics, and so on.

The piccolo solo in the last part of the trio is very well known. Listen for its shrill sound, piping high above the rest of the band.

Sousa once said that his marches were "music for the feet instead of the head." Would you agree? Why?

Down in the Valley

Kentucky Folk Song
Arranged by Kurt Miller

This song is one of the best-known American folk songs. It was originally from the southern Appalachian mountains, but versions of it may now be found all over the country. Is this the version you know? If not, in what ways is it different? Compare it to the modern folk song on the next page. How do you know it is a song of now?

1. Down in the val - ley, the val - ley so low, ___ Hang your head
2. Ros - es love sun - shine, ___ vio - lets love dew, ___ An - gels in
3. Writ - ing a let - ter con - tain - ing three lines, ___ Ask - ing a

(Melody)

o - ver, hear the wind blow. ___ Hear the wind blow, dear, hear the wind
heav - en know I love you, ___ Know I love you, dear, know I love
ques - tion, will you be mine? ___ Will you be mine, dear, will you be

blow, ___ Hang your head o - ver, hear the wind blow. ___
you, ___ An - gels in heav - en know I love you. ___
mine? ___ Ask - ing a ques - tion, will you be mine? ___

I May Not Pass This Way Again

Words and Music
by Rod McKuen

Moderately

1. I'm (we're) on my way____ to find a friend,____
2. I'm (we're) off to find____ that jour - ney's end,____
3. Let's live the day____ un - til its end,____

And I may not pass this way a - gain.____
And I may not pass this way a - gain.____
'Cause we may not pass this way a - gain.____

So let's go build the bridg - es, mis - ter;
So let's go run the ridg - es, mis - ter;
So let's go climb the moun - tains, mis - ter;

Let's go pick the flow - ers, sis - ter.
Let's go find the rain - bow, sis - ter.
Drink from a bub - blin' foun - tain, sis - ter.

Come a - long, strang - er, come a - long friend,

I may not pass this way a - gain.____

What is Music?

You have heard music all of your life. You have studied it in school. You have made up music of your own. You have heard many different sounds, yet they were all called "music." Have you ever wondered why?

Listen to the examples discussed on the following pages. Find other examples and listen to them. Why do we call them all music? In what ways are the examples alike? How are they different?

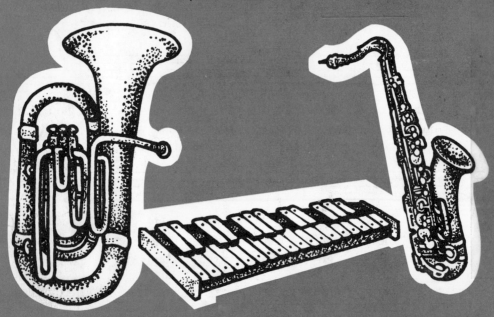

Here are some words that describe the **elements** of music and the way these elements are organized. Did you use any of these terms in your discussion? If you are not sure of the meaning of any of the words, look them up in the dictionary. Listen again to the musical examples and decide whether the terms should be included in your definition of music.

sound	melody	texture
silence	pitch	expression
rhythm	harmony	style
duration	dynamics	design
tempo	timbre (tone color)	

Canon for String Quartet

by Arnold Schoenberg

This music uses something old and something new. The form is old; it is a **canon**. The melody is new; it is based on twelve pitches instead of eight. The string instruments play the twelve-pitch pattern in many ways. Sometimes it is played forward, sometimes backward, and sometimes upside down!

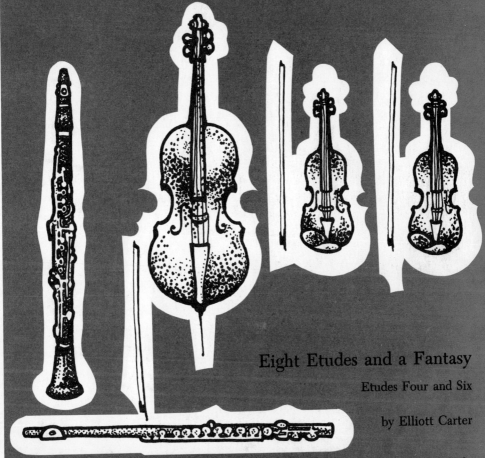

Eight Etudes and a Fantasy

Etudes Four and Six

by Elliott Carter

Listen to "Etude No. 4." "Etude" is a French word which means study. Only one interval is used in the entire composition. How does the composer keep the music interesting?

Listen to "Etude No. 6." How many tones are used? What music elements are altered?

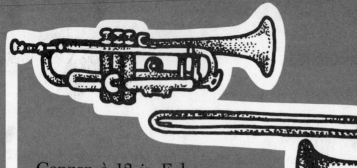

Canzon à 12 in Echo

by Giovanni Gabrieli

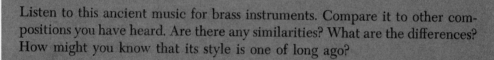

Listen to this ancient music for brass instruments. Compare it to other compositions you have heard. Are there any similarities? What are the differences? How might you know that its style is one of long ago?

Fragment

by Bülent Arel

This music is different from most that you know because all the sounds are electronically produced on an **electronic synthesizer**. Do any of the **timbres** you hear sound like traditional instrumental sounds? Are the musical elements organized differently from traditional music? Is the music similar in any way to traditional music? Compare the style of this music with that of "Canzon à 12 in Echo."

No. 9 Zyklus for One Percussionist

by Karlheinz Stockhausen

Listen to this composition for thirteen percussion instruments and one performer. Look at a page from the **score**. It is in a new kind of notation. Many
contemporary composers feel that traditional notation does not allow them
to express clearly all the directions they wish to give to the performer.
They have had to experiment with new musical symbols.

In this score the performer may begin anywhere he wishes. He may read
the music right side up or upside down! Because of this freedom, the music
sounds new each time it is played.

Develop your own new notation. Can you find a new way to show the
sounds you want played and the duration of each sound? What other instructions must you give in your musical score?

Write a composition using your new notation. Give it to other members of
the class to perform. Did it sound as you intended? Were your instructions
understood?

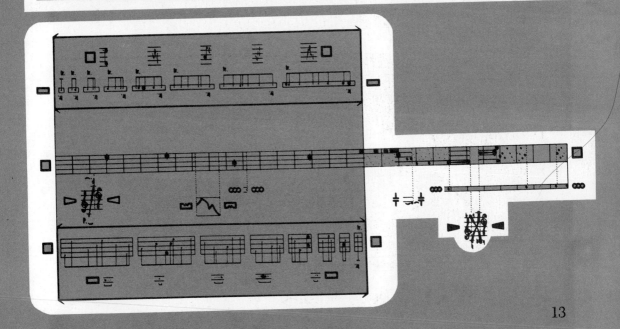

Toembaï

Israeli Round

Fast, with marked rhythm

1. Toem - baï, toem-baï, toem - baï, toem - baï, toem - baï, toem - baï, toem - baï.

2. Tra - la - la, la - la - la - la - la, la - la - la - la - la - la.

3. Tra - la - la - la - la, la - la - la - la - la, la - la - la - la - la - la.

Music Alone Shall Live

German Round

1. All things shall per - ish un - der the sky.

2. Mu - sic a - lone shall live, Mu - sic a - lone shall live,

3. Mu - sic a - lone shall live, nev - er to die.

14

NOTES ON RHYTHM

Make up a rhythm pattern.

Devise your own notation to show how the pattern should sound.

Your notation should give the following information.

1. The relationship of **one sound** to the next.
   How much longer is it? How much shorter is it?

2. The relationship of each sound to a **steady beat**.

3. The **number of beats** that should be grouped together.

Give your notation to a friend. Can he play it correctly?

Here is a rhythm pattern shown in a new notation.
Can you find out the information you need?
Can you perform the pattern on a percussion instrument?
Each space represents a note.

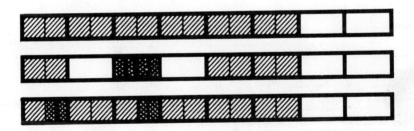

Can you chant or clap the rhythm of "Toembaï"?
How can you find out the information you need from traditional notation?

Can you show the rhythm pattern of "Music Alone Shall Live"
in the new notational scheme shown above?
What will you have to change to make it fit the music?

Go Down the Wishin' Road

Calypso Folk Song
Words and Music Arranged
by Albert Stanton, Jessie Cavanaugh,
and Blake Alphonso Higgs

Calypso music, which began in the West Indies, is also popular in the United States.

Clap each of these patterns several times. How are the patterns different? The second one is an example of **syncopation**.

Listen to the recording and tap the beat. Listen for other syncopated patterns in measures three, five, and ten. Define syncopation.

Notice the interesting accompaniment on the recording. Make up your own percussion accompaniment for this calypso tune. Be sure to include some syncopated patterns.

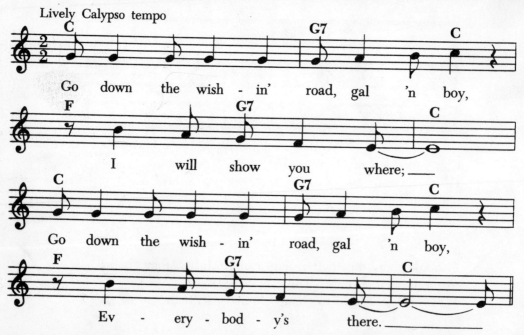

Lively Calypso tempo

Go down the wish - in' road, gal 'n boy,

I will show you where; ___

Go down the wish - in' road, gal 'n boy,

Ev - ery - bod - y's there. ___

16

Allelujah, Amen

Traditional

This melody is based on **a major scale**. Can you decide which one? To do so, find the **key** by looking at the **key signature**. Notice the sharps. **The last sharp is the seventh step of the scale.** Can you locate the first step? The letter name of that pitch is the name of the scale.

Sing the song with numbers. Sing it with words. Sing it as a round.

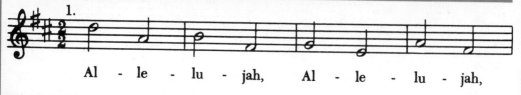

Al - le - lu - jah,   Al - le - lu - jah,

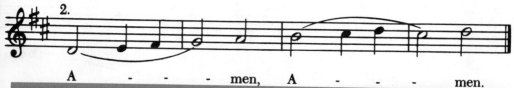

A - - - men,   A - - - men.

Play the melody of this round on the bells. Can you also play it in the keys represented by these key signatures?

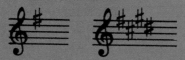

Why are different sharps needed in each key signature? To decide, put the bells in this order and play the scales of G, D, and E.

Notice that sometimes you played bells that were next to each other. This is a **half step**. Sometimes you skipped one bell. This is a **whole step**. Make a diagram showing the sequence of whole and half steps that you played.

Hear the Rooster Crowing

Israeli Round

Look at "Hear the Rooster Crowing." It is based on the E♭ major scale. On what step of the scale is the last flat in the key signature?

Sing the song with numbers. Sing the song with words. Sing it as a round.

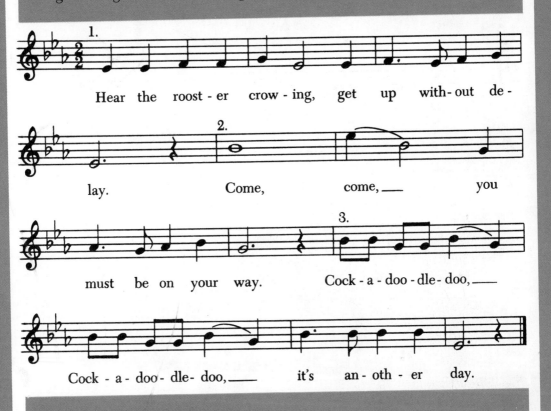

Hear the roost-er crow-ing, get up with-out de-lay. Come, come, ___ you must be on your way. Cock-a-doo-dle-doo, ___ Cock-a-doo-dle-doo, ___ it's an-oth-er day.

Play the song on the bells in the key of E flat. Play it in these keys.

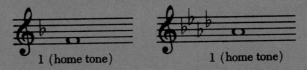

1 (home tone)   1 (home tone)

Make up a rule for finding the key when the key signature is in flats.

Tina Singu

African Folk Song

The song on this page and those on pages 22 through 31 are songs from foreign lands. People from these countries have immigrated to America, bringing their music with them.

LEADER
Ti - na sing - u le - lu - vu - tae - o.

GROUP
Wat - sha, Wat - sha, Wat - sha,

LEADER
Ti - na!

GROUP
Ti - na sing - u

le - lu - vu - tae - o. Wat - sha, Wat - sha,

1. Wat - sha,

2. Wat - sha.

LOWER VOICES
La - la - la - la - la

HIGHER VOICES
Wat - sha, _____ Wat - sha, _____

la, la - la - la - la - la - la, la - la - la - la - la -

Wat - sha,   Wat - sha,   Wat - sha, _____

la,   la - la - la - la - la - la,   la - la - la - la - la -

Wat - sha, _____   Wat - sha, _____

la,   la - la - la - la - la   la,   la - la - la - la - la -

Wat - sha,   Wat - sha,   Wat - sha.

la,   la - la - la - la - la - la.

Experiment with these rhythm patterns as you sing "Tina Singu."

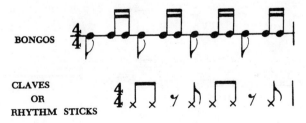

BONGOS

CLAVES
OR
RHYTHM STICKS

La Bamba

Mexican Folk Melody
English Words by Elena Paz

This dance tune is enjoyed by Spanish-speaking people all over the Western Hemisphere. When you know the music, some of you may wish to dance while others sing.

22

gra - cia, _____ u - na po - ca de
sway - ing, _____ Yes the rhy - thm is

¡Bam - ba, bam - ba! _____

gra - cia yo - tra co - si - ta! ¡Ya - rri - ba, a-
sway - ing, your heart feels gay! Sing a - rri - ba, a-

¡Bam - ba, bam - ba! _____

rri - ba, _____ Y a - rri - ba, a-
rri - ba, _____ Sing a - rri - ba, a-

¡Y a - rri - ba, _____
Sing a - rri - ba, _____

ne - ro, _____   yo no soy ma - ri -
Bam - ba, _____   When you're danc - ing the

¡A - rri - ba!
Bam - ba!

ne - ro, por ti se - ré, por ti se -
Bam - ba, you can't go wrong, you can't go

¡A - rri - ba, por ti se -
Bam - ba, you can't go

ré, por ti se - ré!   ¡Bam - ba! _____
wrong, you can't go wrong!   Bam - ba! _____

ré, por ti se - ré! _____ ¡Bam - ba! _____
wrong, you can't go wrong! _____ Bam - ba! _____

25

Kalinka

Russian Folk Song

Refrain

Ka - lin - ka, ka lin - ka, ka - lin - ka of mine!

1.
In the gar - den grows a ber - ry like sweet sher - ry wine. Ka -

2. Fine

Verse

wine. Oh, ___ 1. Un - der the _ pine tree, un - der the _ green tree,
2. Lit - tle ___ pine tree, thou _ ev - er - green tree,

There I'll ___ lay ___ me ___ down to sleep. Ah!
With your ___ rus - tling ___ do not wake me.

Ay, ___ liu - li, liu - li, ay, ___ liu - li, ___
Ay, ___ liu - li, liu - li, ay, ___ liu - li, ___

Dal 𝄋 al Fine

There I'll ___ lay ___ me ___ down to sleep. Ka -
With your ___ rus - tling ___ do not wake me. Ka -

Traditional Round

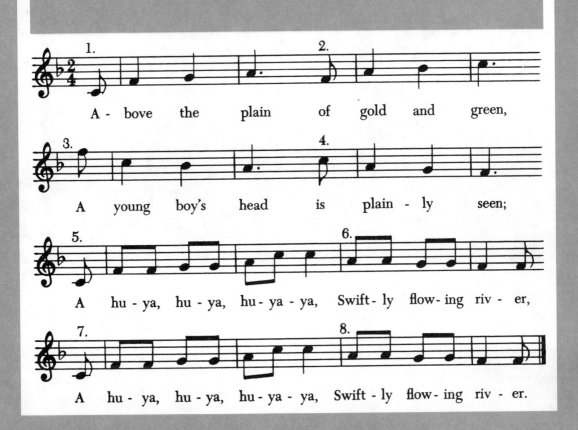

A - bove the plain of gold and green,

A young boy's head is plain - ly seen;

A hu - ya, hu - ya, hu - ya - ya, Swift - ly flow - ing riv - er,

A hu - ya, hu - ya, hu - ya - ya, Swift - ly flow - ing riv - er.

The round may be sung in as many as eight parts. Begin by dividing your class into two groups, then into four. When you know the melody very well, try it in eight parts. Another time, some of you may sing or play this **ostinato**, or chant, as an accompaniment.

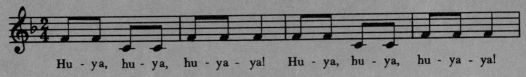

Hu - ya, hu - ya, hu - ya - ya! Hu - ya, hu - ya, hu - ya - ya!

Song of the Three "Nots"

Chinese Folk Song
English Words by Betty Warner Dietz
and Thomas Choobai Park

This song is based on a **pentatonic scale.**

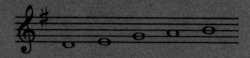

Compare this scale with the major and minor scales you know.

Improvise an accompaniment on bells or flute. Use patterns from the song.

Briskly

1. Kwei Cho's moun-tains are so high,_____
2. Kwei Cho's moun-tains are so high,_____
3. Kwei Cho's moun-tains are so high,_____

Love-ly green_ moun-tains ris-ing_ sharp-ly,
Moss-cov-ered moun-tains ris-ing_ sharp-ly;
Tall,_ green_ moun-tains rich_ with_ min-'rals;

For-ests grow on east and west slopes,
Pour-ing rain fills rush-ing streams._____
Moun-tain folk are sol-diers or min-ers,

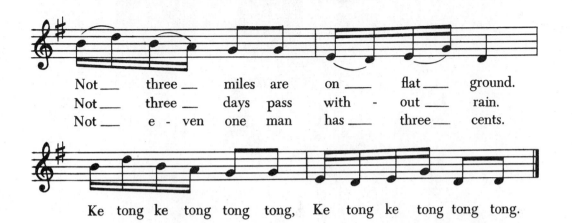

Not three miles are on flat ground.
Not three days pass with-out rain.
Not e-ven one man has three cents.

Ke tong ke tong tong tong, Ke tong ke tong tong tong.

Valleys Green, You Are My Joy

German Folk Melody
Words by Beth Landis

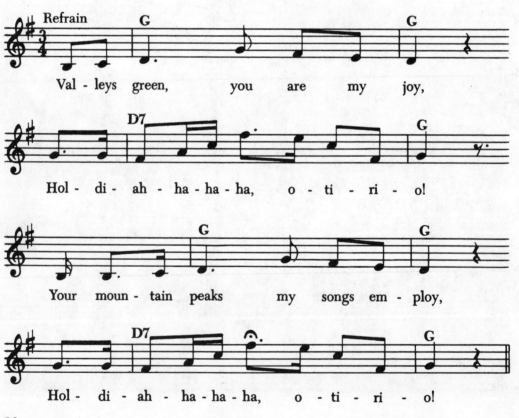

Val - leys green, you are my joy,

Hol - di - ah - ha - ha - ha, o - ti - ri - o!

Your moun - tain peaks my songs em - ploy,

Hol - di - ah - ha - ha - ha, o - ti - ri - o!

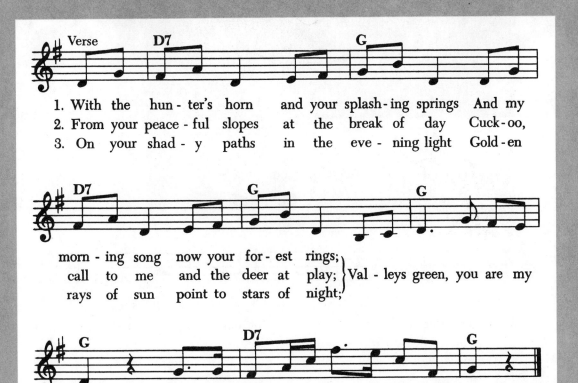

1. With the hun-ter's horn and your splash-ing springs And my
2. From your peace-ful slopes at the break of day Cuck-oo,
3. On your shad-y paths in the eve-ning light Gold-en

morn-ing song now your for-est rings;
call to me and the deer at play; } Val-leys green, you are my
rays of sun point to stars of night;

joy, Hol-di-ah-ha-ha-ha, o-ti-ri-o!

Play the descant on the bells. Someone who is studying flute or violin might play it an octave higher on his instrument.

31

On Top of Old Smoky

Kentucky Folk Song

1. On top of Old Smok - y _____ All cov - ered with snow, _____
2. O court - ing's a pleas - ure, _____ But part - ing's a grief, _____
3. A thief will but rob you _____ Of all that you save, _____
4. The grave will de - cay you _____ And turn you to dust, _____

I lost my true lov - er _____ By court - ing too slow. _____
And a false - heart - ed lov - er _____ Is worse than a thief. _____
But a false - heart - ed lov - er _____ Sends you to your grave. _____
But a false - heart - ed lov - er _____ You nev - er can trust. _____

Plan your own instrumental accompaniment for this song. Begin by discovering the chord that should be used to accompany the melody in each measure. You will need these chords.

I   IV   V7

Look at the notes in the first measure. To which chord do all of the tones belong? Use that chord to accompany the melody of that measure. Follow the same procedure and determine the chords for each measure in the song.

When you have discovered the sequence of chords, play them on the autoharp, bells, or piano. Accompany the class as it sings.

When you know the chords that harmonize a melody, you can use the information in many ways.

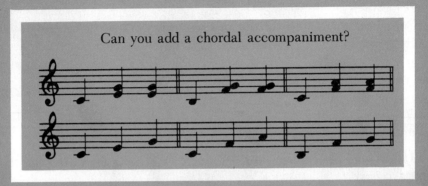

Can you add a chordal accompaniment?

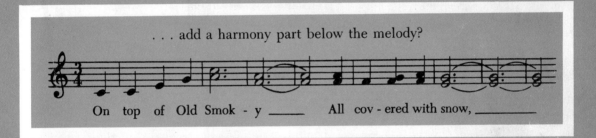

. . . add a harmony part below the melody?

On top of Old Smok - y _____ All cov - ered with snow, _____

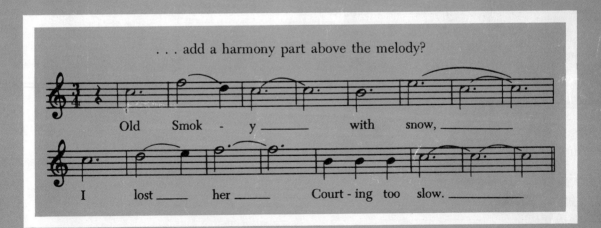

. . . add a harmony part above the melody?

Old Smok - y _____ with snow, _____

I lost _____ her _____ Court - ing too slow. _____

Battle Hymn of the Republic

Music Attributed to William Steffe
Words by Julia Ward Howe

Study the notation. Listen to the recording. Notice the different ways the melody is harmonized. Do you hear any of the ways that were discussed on pages 32-33?

Mine eyes have seen the glo - ry of the com - ing of the Lord;

He is tram - pling out the vin - tage where the grapes of wrath are stored;

He hath loosed the fate - ful light - ning of his ter - ri - ble swift sword;

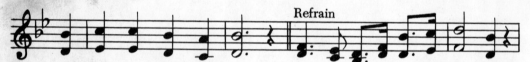

Refrain

His truth is march - ing on. Glo - ry, glo - ry, hal - le - lu - jah!

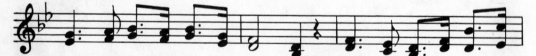

Glo - ry, glo - ry, hal - le - lu - jah! Glo - ry, glo - ry, hal - le -

lu - jah! His truth is march - ing on.

Listen for the descant sung by a soprano voice. Some people in the class may sing the descant while others sing the melody.

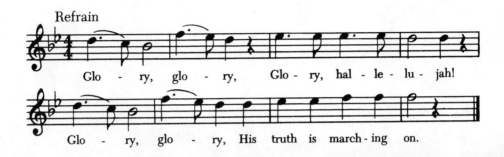

Refrain

Glo - ry, glo - ry, Glo - ry, hal - le - lu - jah!

Glo - ry, glo - ry, His truth is march - ing on.

HEAR DESIGN...
SHOW DESIGN

Concerto No. 25, "Water Music Suite"

Allegro, Bourrée, Hornpipe, and Allegro Deciso

by George Frideric Handel
Arranged by Sir Hamilton Harty

A design may be made up of parts that are the same and parts that are different.

Listen to four short dances.
Talk about the ways that the parts are combined to form a complete design.

FIRST DANCE: Which of these words suggests the design?

an echo   a mirror   an argument

SECOND DANCE: Could any of the words above describe the design of this dance? Can you think of a better descriptive term?

THIRD DANCE: Woodwinds begin this dance. When each new section begins, which of these words best describes what happens to the **instrumentation?**

more   less   different   same

FOURTH DANCE: Which set of letters best describes the design?

A B C D   A B B   A B A

Work in pairs. Choose one of the dances.
Plan a way to show its design.
    Show it in dance movements.
    Show it with lines, colors, and shapes.
    Show it by composing your own music in the same design.

An Event for SIX Players

What would happen if . . .

you played the events in this circle?

Choose any order. Try going **faster** when the staff goes **up** and **slower** when it goes **down**.

Think about which instruments you will choose.
Will you play with *legato* or *staccato* sounds?
Will all the instruments play all the time?
Will they start and stop at different times?

Music of the Eastern Seaboard

The English people who first settled this land came from a country which had a well-developed musical life. They knew and loved music. The New England settlers continued to sing hymns and folk songs as they were busy building new homes and new lives. As people arrived from France, Germany, Sweden, and other European countries, other musicians began to perform and to teach music, and American composers began to write their own compositions.

Metropolitan areas such as New York City, Philadelphia, and Boston became centers of musical life. World-famous orchestras and opera companies exist in these and other eastern cities.

People from other lands continue to arrive in the cities along the eastern seaboard. Today one can hear the music of Puerto Rico, Cuba, and Jamaica as well as the songs of Europe, Africa, and the Far East in many of our cities.

American composers and performers have been influenced by the types of music which can be heard. They have taken musical ideas from many sources and developed new forms. Young musicians in all sections of the country are making their own music and creating new styles of folk and popular music. Music in America constantly grows and changes, just as our country continues to grow and change.

Old Hundredth

Music Attributed to
Louis Bourgeois
Words by Thomas Ken

"Old Hundredth," based on Psalm 100, first appeared in the "Bay Psalm Book." This was the first book printed in America.

Praise God from whom all bless - ings flow;

Praise him, all crea - tures here be - low;

Praise him a - bove, ye heav'n - ly host:

Praise Fa - ther, Son, and Ho - ly Ghost.

Listen to the recording. You will hear four arrangements of this melody. The first arrangement is played by instruments alone. Which instrument plays first? Then you will hear the four-part harmonization sung by a choir. The third arrangement was written by John Dowland, an English composer who lived during the time of the Puritans. Compare it to the fourth arrangement made by a contemporary composer.

40

COLONIAL ORGAN MUSIC

The President's March

by Philip Phile

The pipe organ was one of the first musical instruments built in America. Many early organs have been preserved and reconstructed.

The "President's March" has continued to be played on grand occasions since it was first used at the inauguration of George Washington.

Listen to the music. Determine its design. The music was originally written for instruments. Later, words were added and the song was known as "Hail Columbia." It was our first national anthem.

Fugue in D Major

by William Selby

This music was also composed during Washington's time. Listen to the **fugue** as played on the organ in the Old North Church in Boston. The **fugue** is a common musical design. It is based on a main theme called the **subject**. The subject is stated in different voices, somewhat like a round.

Listen to the music. After the subject is played, it enters again three times, each time in a lower voice. Listen for **episodes**, that is, sections in which new ideas are introduced or old ones developed. How does the fugue close?

A-Roving

Sea Chantey
Arranged by Kurt Miller

1. In Plym-outh town there lived a maid, Mark well what I do say.
2. I took this fair maid for a walk, Mark well what I do say.
3. But when my cash was gone and spent, Mark well what I do say.

In Plym-outh town there lived a maid Of beau-ty rare, and so I stayed;
I took this fair maid for a walk. And we did have a love-ly talk;
But when my cash was gone and spent, Then this fair maid, a - way she went;

I'll go no more a - rov - ing with you, fair maid.

Refrain

A - rov - ing, a - rov - ing, a - rov - ing's my ruin.

(Melody)

A - rov - ing, a - rov - ing since rov - ing's been my ru - i - in,

I'll go no more 'rov - ing with you, fair maid.

I'll go no more a - rov - ing with you, fair maid.

42

Lumberjack Song

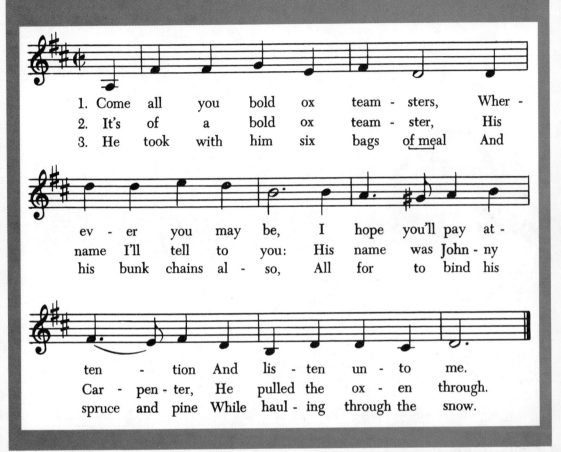

1. Come all you bold ox team - sters, Wher -
2. It's of a bold ox team - ster, His
3. He took with him six bags of meal And

ev - er you may be, I hope you'll pay at -
name I'll tell to you: His name was John - ny
his bunk chains al - so, All for to bind his

ten - tion And lis - ten un - to me.
Car - pen - ter, He pulled the ox - en through.
spruce and pine While haul - ing through the snow.

4. Says Carpenter unto Flemmons,
"I'll show them to haul spruce,
For my oxen in the snow, you see,
Are equal to bull moose!"

5. Now the crew that tend those oxen,
Their names to you I'll tell:
The jobber's name was Crowley—
The boys all knew him well.

6. Old Duke and Swan all on the pole,
So vigorous they do lug,
While Swan's the head with a collar
    and hames
And a pair of leather tugs.

7. Old Brighty in the hovel lay,
They say his feet are sore.
But it was a strain that caused
    his pain,
And now he'll haul no more.

Shenandoah

American Sea Chantey

Compare the words and music of this American sea chantey with "A-Roving."
In what ways are the two chanteys similar? How are they different?

1. Oh, Shen - an - doah, ___ I long to hear you,
2. Oh, Shen - an - doah, ___ I love your daugh - ter,
3. Oh, Shen - an - doah, ___ I'm bound to leave you,

A - way, you roll - in' riv - er,

Oh, Shen - an - doah, ___ I long to hear you,
Oh, Shen - an - doah, ___ I love your daugh - ter,
Oh, Shen - an - doah, ___ I'm bound to leave you,

A - way I'm bound to go, 'Cross the wide Mis - sour - i.

44

Sea Chantey

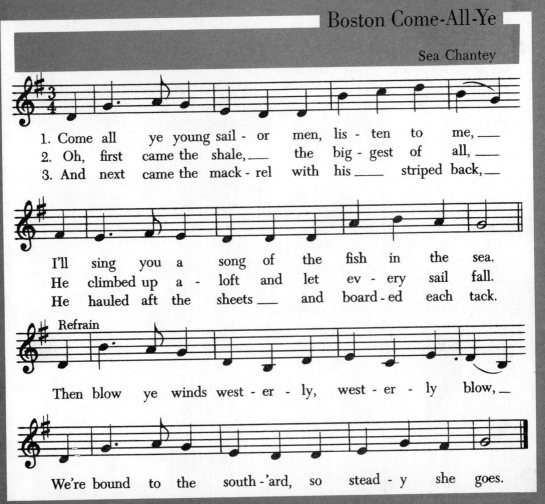

1. Come all ye young sail-or men, lis-ten to me, ___
2. Oh, first came the shale, ___ the big-gest of all, ___
3. And next came the mack-rel with his ___ striped back, ___

I'll sing you a song of the fish in the sea.
He climbed up a-loft and let ev-ery sail fall.
He hauled aft the sheets ___ and board-ed each tack.

Refrain

Then blow ye winds west-er-ly, west-er-ly blow, ___

We're bound to the south-'ard, so stead-y she goes.

4. Then came the smelt, the smallest of all;
   He jumped to the poop and sang out, "Top-sail haul!"
   Then blow ye . . . .

5. Last came the flounder, as flat as the ground,
   Says, "Blast your eyes, chuckle-head, mind how you sound!"
   Then blow ye . . . .

Sing this descant with the refrain of the song or play it on the bells.

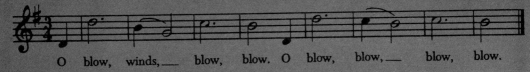

O blow, winds, ___ blow, blow. O blow, blow, ___ blow, blow.

What has happened to the word in this picture? Can you say this word three different ways to match the pictures?

What has happened to the rhythm in these three patterns? Speak the three rhythm patterns using the words "chairs to mend."

Which of these patterns do you find in the song? Could you perform the song in **diminution**? Which of the three patterns would you use? Now could you perform it in **augmentation**? Try combining two or three versions at the same time.

Chairs to Mend

Traditional Round

Chester

from *New England Triptych*

by William Schuman

Learn to sing this melody. It was composed as a hymn. During the Revolutionary War it was sung to patriotic words. The song became a popular marching song.

Chant the words of the song in the rhythm shown. Can you chant them in diminution? in augmentation?

Now listen to a composition by William Schuman. As you listen, notice ways Schuman has changed the music of the hymn and used it with his own musical material. Listen for changes in melody, rhythm and harmony. Listen for different instruments.

Erie Canal

American Work Song

Study the rhythm. What is the meter? What note sounds with the beat? Locate syncopated patterns. Find patterns in the refrain that include dotted notes. Practice clapping these patterns. Be sure that the dotted note is **three times as long** as the note that follows it.

1. I   got   a   mule, her   name is   Sal,   Fif - teen   miles on the
2. Git   up there, Sal, we passed that lock,   Fif - teen   miles on the

E - rie Ca - nal! __ She's a   good old work-er and a good old   pal,
E - rie Ca - nal! __ And __ we'll make Rome be- fore __ six   o - 'clock,

Fif - teen   miles on the   E - rie Ca-nal! __ We've hauled some barg- es
Fif - teen   miles on the   E - rie Ca-nal! __ Just one   more trip and

48

in our day, Filled with lum- ber, coal, and hay, And we know ev - ery
back we'll go Through the rain and sleet and snow, 'Cause we know ev - ery

inch of the way From Al - ba- ny ___ to ___ Buf - fa - lo. ___
inch of the way From Al - ba- ny ___ to ___ Buf - fa - lo. ___

Refrain

Low bridge, ev- er-y-bod-y down, Low bridge,'cause we're com-ing to a town;

And you'll al - ways know your neigh-bor, You'll al - ways know your pal,

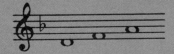 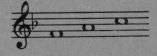

If you ev - er nav - i - gat - ed on the E - rie Ca - nal. ___

Compare the melody of the verse with that of the refrain. Notice that the
two melodies center around different groups of pitches.

The verse centers around: The refrain centers around:

The verse is based on the D minor scale. The refrain is based on the F major
scale. Play the two scales. Why do they have the same key signature?

Simple Gifts

Shaker Song

In the 1700's a religious group called the "Shaking Quakers" or "Shakers" lived in New England. They were simple, pious people who lived according to strict rules. Their name came from the custom of dramatizing their songs through dance.

'Tis the gift to be sim - ple, 'tis the gift to be free, 'Tis the

gift to come down where you ought to be, And when we find our -

selves in the place just right, 'Twill be in the val - ley of

love and de - light. When true sim - pli - ci - ty is gained, To

bow and to bend we shan't be a - shamed, To turn, turn will

be our de - light, Till by turn - ing, turn - ing we come round right.

Shakers Dance

Haymaker's Jig

New England Contradance

A contradance is a dance of contrary motion. Dancers form lines that move in opposite directions. Sometimes it is called the "longways dance" or "line dance" or "string dance." One of the oldest forms of folk dancing, it was brought to the colonies from the British Isles where it was very popular in the seventeenth century. The colonists loved to dance the contras. Even today they are still very popular with folk dancers in our country, especially in New England. Contradances are danced today much as they were three hundred years ago.

A few basic calls are used in contradances. These include "Balance and Swing," "Four-in-Line," "Come Back Up," "Ladies Chain," and others. Choose a leader to shout some calls. Take the dance formation and dance the complete contradance.

51

Altwiener Tanzlied

Austrian Folk Song

This song and the ones on the following pages were brought by people from their European homelands.

The German words for verses 1 and 2 mean:

People do not really need everything they want. Possessions do not bring happiness anyway, because when people do get everything they want, they usually are miserable.

1. Nein,   nein,   nein, a - ber nein!   Im - mer - zu kann man nicht,
2. Ja,   ja,   ja, a - ber ja!   Wenn die Leut' gran - tig sein,

Wenn man will, darf man nicht. Nein,   nein,   nein, a - ber nein!
Schiebt man s'i'n O - fen 'nein. Ja,   ja,   ja, a - ber ja!

Im - mer - zu kann man nicht lu - stig sein.
Schiebt man s'i'n O - fen 'nein und   heizt ein.

Follow the suggestions on page 32. Determine the chords needed to harmonize each measure. Add an autoharp accompaniment. Play in a waltz rhythm. Use one long stroke and two short strokes to each measure.

Riding Together

Czechoslovakian Folk Melody
English words by Beth Landis

The design of the melody is made up of a number of short patterns or **motives**.
Some are one measure long.

Some are two measures.

Notice that sometimes the motives are repeated exactly. Sometimes the
rhythm or melody of the motive is changed in some way.

1. Comes a - rid - ing   in the morn - ing,   up   to   the   gar - den _ gate,
2. In   the win - ter,   in the sum - mer,   for   him   I   glad- ly _ wait,

Hear the hoof - beats, hear the bri - dle,   he's   nev - er   late!
Hear the hoof - beats, hear the bri - dle,   he's   nev - er   late!

Rid- ing, rid - ing we   to - geth - er   go,   Jin-gling o'er the crunch-ing snow,
Rid- ing, rid - ing we   to - geth - er   go,   Val - leys our _   mu - sic know,

Rid - ing,   rid - ing   we   to - geth - er   sing,   Ring, ech - o,   ring!
Rid - ing,   rid - ing   we   to - geth - er   sing,   Ring, ech - o,   ring!

53

Marianina

Italian Folk Song

Compare phrases one and two. Notice that the second phrase imitates the first phrase, one step higher. This is called a **sequence**. Can you find another sequence in the song?

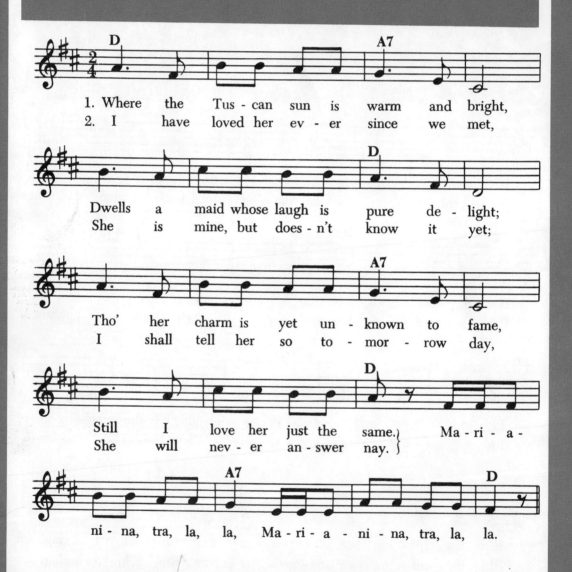

1. Where the Tus - can sun is warm and bright,
2. I have loved her ev - er since we met,

Dwells a maid whose laugh is pure de - light;
She is mine, but does - n't know it yet;

Tho' her charm is yet un - known to fame,
I shall tell her so to - mor - row day,

Still I love her just the same.⎫ Ma - ri - a -
She will nev - er an - swer nay. ⎭

ni - na, tra, la, la, Ma - ri - a - ni - na, tra, la, la.

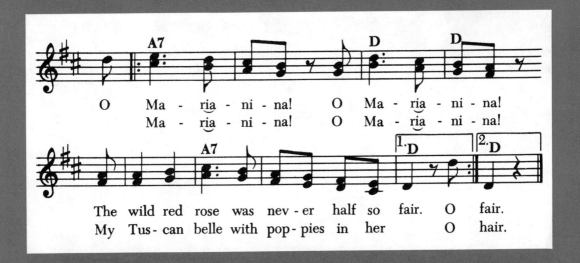

O Ma - ria - ni - na! O Ma - ria - ni - na!
Ma - ria - ni - na! O Ma - ria - ni - na!

The wild red rose was nev - er half so fair. O fair.
My Tus - can belle with pop - pies in her O hair.

Add an accompaniment on the tambourine for the refrain.

Buon giorno

Italian Round

Buon gior - no, mi - a ca - ra bam - bi - na, mol - ti ba - ci,

Buon gior - no, mi - a ca - ra bam - bi - na, mol - ti ba - ci,

Buon gior - no, mi - a ca - ra bam - bi - na, mol - ti ba - ci!

My Wagon

Netherlands Folk Song
Translation by Beth Landis

Chant the words in rhythm. As you chant, someone may tap the accents lightly on a tambourine. Be sure to observe the changing meter.

1. O my wag-on is well-lad-en, full of scold-ing wom-en,
2. O my wag-on is well-lad-en, full of schem-ing grand-dads,
3. O my wag-on is well-lad-en, full of fair young la-dies,

O they quar-rel and they chat-ter, peace I'm nev-er giv-en;
O they're plot-ting and they're plant-ing, how I tire of those lads;
O they're sing-ing and they're chat-ting, and their smiles do me please;

Nev-er a-gain I'll take, for my part, Chat-ter-ing wom-en
Nev-er a-gain I'll take, for my part, Schem-ing old grand-dads
Now once a-gain I'll take, for my part, Fair-est young la-dies

in my horse-cart! Hup, horse, get up!
in my horse-cart! Hup, horse, get up!
in my horse-cart! Hup, horse, get up!

Why is more than one meter signature used? To help you decide, chant the words throughout in $\frac{3}{4}$ meter. Chant in $\frac{2}{4}$ meter.

Oleana

Norwegian Folk Song
Arranged by Kurt Miller
English Words by Beth Landis

Refrain

O - le, O - le,   O - le, O - le,

(Melody)

O - le, O - le - an - a,   O - le, O - le - an - a,

Fine

O - le, O - le,   O - le, O - le - an - a.

O - le, O - le,   O - le, O - le,   O - le, O - le - an - a.

Verse

1. O that is where I'd   like to be, There where the   land is   free;
2. The hens lay eggs as   big as rocks, Roost-ers crow like eight-day clocks,
3. The sal - mon leap so   high up there, Hold your ket - tle   in   the air;
4. O come and bring your fid   -   dle, Dance to the mid   -   dle,

D.C. al Fine

Wheat and corn they grow so   high, The tas - sels dust - ing off the sky!
Roast - ed   pigs run   all   a - bout With knives and forks stuck in their snouts!
They'll jump in, pull on   the   lid, And cook them - selves to look like squid!
O - le with his   vi - o - lin Will help us make a mer - ry din!

Putnam's Camp, Redding, Connecticut

from *Three Places* in *New England*

by Charles Ives

The music of "Putnam's Camp" describes the story of a boy who goes to the park for a Fourth of July picnic. He wanders into the woods, then falls asleep and dreams of the old soldiers and their hardships. He awakens and goes back to join the fun.

Listen for the ways the music suggests the sound and mood of a celebration. Follow the "map" below. It shows some "musical landmarks" you will hear as you listen to the first part of the music.

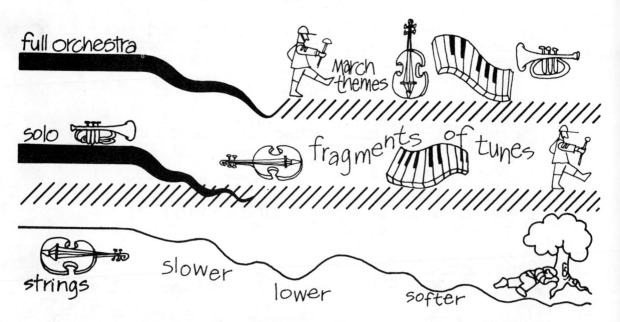

Work together. Make your own musical map of the rest of the music. Put in important musical landmarks that you hear.

The Cage

Words and Music
by Charles Ives

Have you ever watched a caged animal pace back and forth?

Read the poem with no pitch changes in your voice. Add a bell accompaniment as you speak. Use Scale I or Scale II.

Scale 1

A leopard went around his cage from one side to the other side, he stopped only when the keeper came around with meat. A boy who had been there three hours began to wonder—Is-life anything like that?

Scale 2

Listen to the recording of "The Cage," by Charles Ives. In what ways does it resemble your own performance of the song?

59

Experiment with the new ways of organizing music. Use ideas you heard in the compositions of Charles Ives. Work alone or in a small group.

an event for six

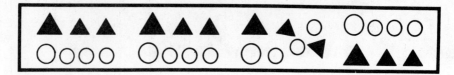

Explore ways of combining music with different meters.

- Divide into two groups. One group may chant or clap the rhythm of "Battle Hymn of the Republic," page 34, while another performs the rhythm of "When Johnny Comes Marching Home," page 6.

- Compose two phrases of rhythm—one in **threes,** another in **twos.** Two people may play the phrases at the same time. Use percussion instruments with contrasting tone qualities.

an event for eight

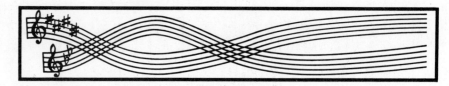

Explore ways of combining music in different keys.

- Can you sing "Battle Hymn of the Republic" and "Simple Gifts," page 50, at the same time?

- Choose two members of the group to play a familiar melody such as "Chairs to Mend," page 46, on two sets of bells. One might play it in the key in which it is written on page 46. The other person might play it in C. (Begin on G.)

an event for one

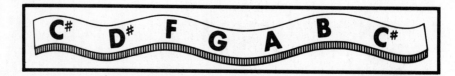

Compose music based on the whole-tone scale.

- Arrange the bells in a whole-tone scale starting on C♯. Play "Are You Sleeping?" in this new scale. (Start on F.)

- Make up a melody of your own. Use only the pitches that belong to a whole-tone scale.

60

Dust of Snow

Music by Arthur Frackenpohl
Words by Robert Frost

The way a crow Shook down on me

The dust of snow From a hem - lock tree

Has giv - en my heart A change of mood

And saved some part Of a day I had rued.

A Minor Bird

by Robert Frost

I have wished a bird would fly away,
And not sing by my house all day:

Have clapped my hands at him from the door
When it seemed as if I could bear no more.

The fault must partly have been in me.
The bird was not to blame for his key.

And of course there must be something wrong
In wanting to silence any song.

61

Guantanamera (Lady of Guantanamo)

Spanish Words by José Marti
English Adaptation by Bernard Gasso

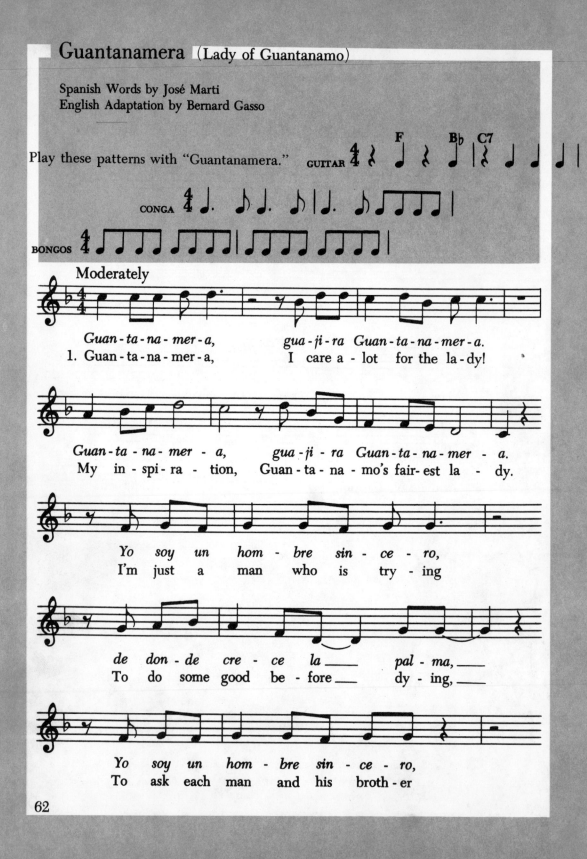

Play these patterns with "Guantanamera."

Moderately

Guan-ta-na-mer-a,   gua-ji-ra Guan-ta-na-mer-a.
1. Guan-ta-na-mer-a,   I care a-lot for the la-dy!

Guan-ta-na-mer-a,   gua-ji-ra Guan-ta-na-mer-a.
My in-spi-ra-tion,   Guan-ta-na-mo's fair-est la-dy.

Yo soy un hom-bre sin-ce-ro,
I'm just a man who is try-ing

de don-de cre-ce la___ pal-ma,___
To do some good be-fore___ dy-ing,___

Yo soy un hom-bre sin-ce-ro,
To ask each man and his broth-er

62

de don-de cre - - ce la pal - ma,____
To bear no ill ____ toward each oth - er. ____

Ya n tes de mor - rir - me quie - ro,
This life will nev - er be hol - low

E - char mis ver - sos del al - ma.
To those who lis - ten and fol - low.

Guan - ta - na - mer - a, gua - ji - ra Guan - ta - na - mer - a.
Guan - ta - na - mer - a, I care a - lot for the la - dy!

Guan - ta - na - mer - a, gua - ji - ra Guan - ta - na - mer - a.
My in - spi - ra - tion, Guan - ta - na - mo's fair - est la - dy.

2. *Guantanamera, guajira Guantanamera.*
    Guantanamera, guajira Guantanamera.
    A little brook on a mountain,
    The cooling spray of a fountain—
    Arouse in me an emotion,
    More than the vast boundless ocean,
    For there's a wealth beyond measure
    In little things that we treasure.
    Guantanamera, guajira Guantanamera.
    Guantanamera, guajira Guantanamera.

This arrangement, with the refrain addressed to a young girl, and the patriotic verses of the great poet, is popular with many Spanish-speaking people.

Lift Every Voice and Sing

Music by J. Rosamund Johnson
Words by James Weldon Johnson

Lift ev - ery voice and sing Till earth and heav - en ring,

Ring with the har - mo - nies of lib - er - ty;

Let our re - joic - ing rise High as the list - 'ning — skies,

Let it re - sound loud as the roll - ing sea.

Sing a song full of the faith that the dark past has taught us,

Sing a song full of the hope that the pres - ent has brought us.

Fac - ing the ris - ing sun Of our new day be - gun,

Let us march on till vic - to - ry _____ is won. _____

Fourteenth of July, Rue Montorgeuil, 1878
by Claude Monet

Shalom, Chaverim

Farewell, Good Friends

Israeli Round

Jewish people from many countries in Europe have come to the United States. Many of their songs, such as the one on this page, have become favorites of Americans of every faith.

Sha - lom, cha - ve - rim! Sha - lom, cha - ve - rim! Sha - lom, sha - lom!
Fare - well, good _ friends, Fare - well, good _ friends, Fare - well, fare - well!

Le - hit - ra - ot, le - hit - ra - ot, Sha - lom, sha - lom!
Till we meet a - gain, till we meet a - gain, Fare - well, fare - well!

This song is based on the E minor scale.

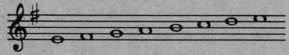

Play the minor scale on the bells. Describe its sequence of whole and half steps.

Compare it to these major scales. What does it have in common with the E major scale? What does it have in common with the G major scale? In what ways is it different from these scales?

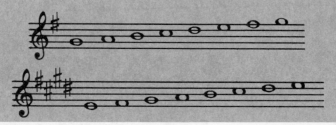

66

BEHIND THE MOON

by B. A.

Chattering cheetahs?
Bewitched, scratching
chasing
and
chopping
and scarily
thrashing!

Grinches
who
twitch
and
mew
and
pitch
over
the
chimney . . .
snicker and snitch!

fooI-MooL
Groan-MoAN
LONG-HOLLOW
LONE—
LONE-

YOUR GAME OF PAIRS

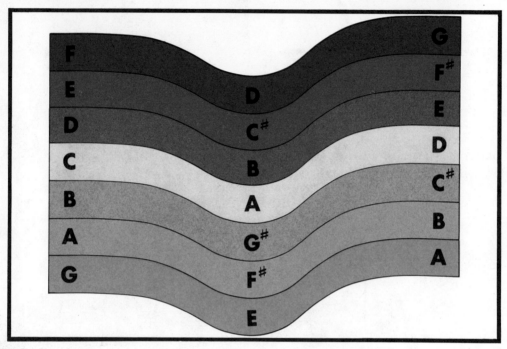

Work in pairs.

- You play "It's Raining" on the lowest set of pitches: G E A. Choose any instrument on which you can play those three tones.

- Your partner plays "It's Raining" at the same time. He chooses another set of pitches.

- Which set will he play if he wants to play at the **interval of a sixth** above you? a **third?** a **seventh?** a **fifth?** a **second?**

- Experiment with different intervals. Listen to the distinctive sound of each.

- Choose a pair of intervals. Play your duet for your classmates. Can they hear which interval you are playing?

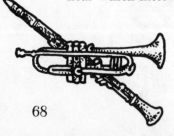

BARTÒK'S GAME OF PAIRS

Concerto for Orchestra, Second Movement

by Béla Bartók

The composer Bartók composed a game of pairs for instruments of the orchestra.

Follow this chart as you listen. Each pair of instruments plays at a different interval. They perform the same intervals you played. Can you identify the interval they play each time?

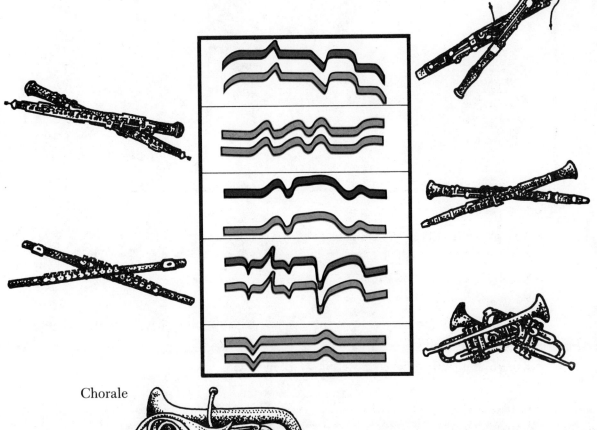

Chorale

What do you hear during the last section of the movement?

Music of the Southland

Music in the South is a colorful mixture of the contributions of the groups that settled there. In the mountain regions the folk songs and ballads of the British Isles have been preserved. Although some of the songs have changed over the years, many are still sung exactly as they were sung centuries ago.

In Louisiana, people from Spain and France brought music from their homelands. Creole music, with its distinctive rhythms and melodies, resulted from a combination of French and Spanish music. It is still alive today. New Orleans became a center of musical life in the South. Many European operas were given their first American performance in the opera house built in New Orleans in 1808.

The African also brought his music to the New World. As he heard the music of the new country, he wove it into his own music. The spirituals, blues, and work songs of the first Afro-Americans have had an important effect on American music. Jazz had its beginning in the blues songs and music of the marching bands in New Orleans. The gospel and soul music of Black Americans is still popular today.

The folk music of the Southland has interested and influenced composers. Nearly a hundred years ago Stephen Foster and Louis Gottschalk wove the rhythms and melodies of southern folk music into their works. Since that time, many other composers have incorporated such musical ideas into their compositions.

Sourwood Mountain

Kentucky Folk Song

Determine the design of this song by studying the notation. Find motives, phrases, sections. How does knowing the design help you learn the music?

Practice clapping the rhythmic motives that you find. If you are not sure how to clap the dotted rhythm, practice this pattern.

1. Chick - en crow - in' on Sour - wood Moun - tain,
2. My true love's ___ a blue - eyed dai - sy,
3. My true love ___ lives up the riv - er,

Hey de - ing dang did - dle al - ly day.
Hey de - ing dang did - dle al - ly day. If
Hey de - ing dang did - dle al - ly day. A

So man - y pret - ty girls, I can't count 'em,
I don't ___ get ___ her, I'll go cra - zy,
few more ___ jumps ___ and I'll be with her,

Hey de - ing dang did - dle al - ly day.
Hey de - ing dang did - dle al - ly day.
Hey de - ing dang did - dle al - ly day.

My true love, she lives in Letch - er,
Big dog bark and lit - tle one bite you,
My true love lives up the hol - ler,

Hey de - ing dang did - dle al - ly day.
Hey de - ing dang did - dle al - ly day.
Hey de - ing dang did - dle al - ly day.

She won't come and I won't fetch her,
Big girl court and lit - tle one slight you,
She won't come and I won't fol - ler,

Hey de - ing dang did - dle al - ly day.
Hey de - ing dang did - dle al - ly day.
Hey de - ing dang did - dle al - ly day.

Hop Up, My Ladies

American Folk Song

Listen to the recording. The accompaniment is played on popular folk instruments. Notice how the melody is passed from harmonica to banjo to fiddle.

1. Did you ev - er go to meet - ing, Un - cle Joe, Un - cle Joe?
2. Will your horse _ car - ry dou - ble, Un - cle Joe, Un - cle Joe?
3. Is your horse a sin - gle foot - er, Un - cle Joe, Un - cle Joe?

Did you ev - er go to meet - ing, Un - cle Joe? _
Will your horse _ car - ry dou - ble, Un - cle Joe? _
Is your horse a sin - gle foot - er, Un - cle Joe? _

Did you ev - er go to meet - ing, Un - cle Joe, Un - cle Joe?
Will your horse _ car - ry dou - ble, Un - cle Joe, Un - cle Joe?
Is your horse a sin - gle foot - er, Un - cle Joe, Un - cle Joe?

Don't mind the weath - er, so the winds don't blow.
Don't mind the weath - er, so the winds don't blow.
Don't mind the weath - er, so the winds don't blow.

Refrain

Hop up, my la - dies, three in a row,

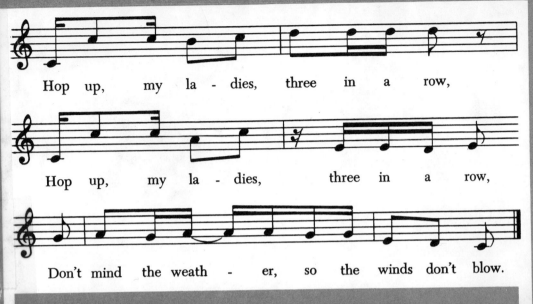

Hop up, my la - dies, three in a row,

Hop up, my la - dies, three in a row,

Don't mind the weath - er, so the winds don't blow.

4. Would you rather own a pacer, Uncle Joe, Uncle Joe?
   Don't mind the weather, so the winds don't blow. *Refrain*

5. Say, you don't want to gallop, Uncle Joe, Uncle Joe.
   Don't mind the weather, so the winds don't blow. *Refrain*

6. Say, you might take a tumble, Uncle Joe, Uncle Joe.
   Don't mind the weather, so the winds don't blow. *Refrain*

7. Well, we'll get there soon as the others, Uncle Joe,
   Don't mind the weather, so the winds don't blow. *Refrain*

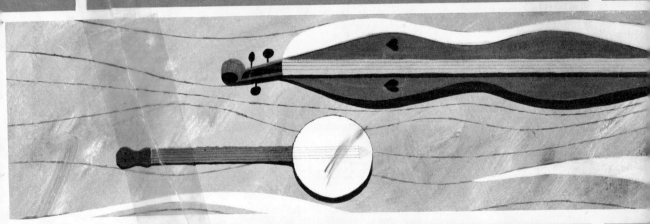

Old Joe Clarke

American Folk Song

This melody was a popular fiddle tune enjoyed by the early American settlers. Compare it with the Irish tune discussed on the next page.

1. Old Joe Clarke he had a house Six - teen sto - ries high;
2. I went down to Old Joe's house, nev-er been there be - fore;

Ev - ery sto - ry in that house Was filled with chick-en pie.
He slept on a feath - er bed And I slept on the floor.

Refrain

Round and round, Old Joe Clarke, Round and round I say;

Round and round, Old Joe Clarke, I have - n't long to stay.

Someone who plays the violin may play this as an introduction to "Old Joe Clarke." Then play the final chord on the first beat of every measure throughout the song.

Folk Instruments of the United States

Folk music played on instruments such as the guitar, banjo, and fiddle has always been popular in this country. Although we usually think of such music as American, the instruments were originally brought from other lands. The violin has long been used in Europe. The guitar dates back at least to the fifteenth century. The banjo's ancestor can be found in Africa.

Listen to "Bird in the Tree," an Irish tune. Notice the style of fiddling. Fiddlers were popular in mountain communities because they could play for community dances. Even today, some communities hold fiddling contests and people come from miles around to compete and enjoy the music. Compare the way the fiddler plays his violin in "Bird in the Tree" with other violin music you have heard.

"Nothing to It" is in the style known today as "country music." Listen for solos on the banjo, guitar, fiddle, and harmonica. You will hear a bass guitar as well as a steel guitar which has a sound similar to the Hawaiian guitar.

Farewell, My Own True Love

American Folk Song
Collected by William S. Haynie

The melodies of many ballads and songs from the hills and mountains of the Southeast are very old. Many originated in England. Often they are based on scales that are unfamiliar to us. Listen to the songs on this page and the next. Notice that the melody seems to be neither major nor minor. It moves back and forth between the two. These melodies are really based on **modes**, scales which originated in ancient times.

1. Fare - well, my own true love,
2. Ten thou - sand mile, my love,
3. Oh, don't you see that dove

Fare - well a lit - tle while,
Through Eng - land, France, and Spain;
That flies from vine to vine,

I'm goin' a - way but I'll come a - gain,
My rov - ing mind shall __ nev - er rest
A - mourn - ing for his __ own true love,

If I go ten thou - sand mile.
Till I see your face a - gain.
Just as I will mourn for mine.

Riddles

Kentucky Folk Song

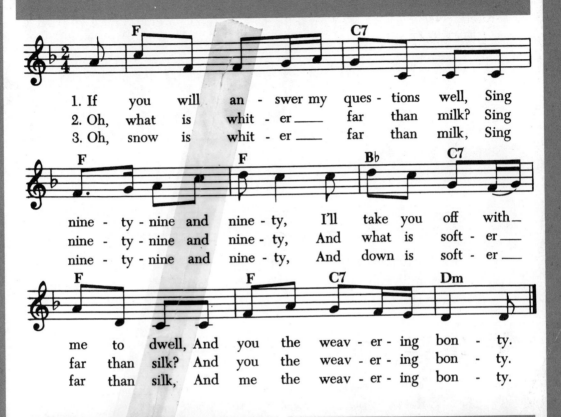

1. If you will an - swer my ques - tions well, Sing
2. Oh, what is whit - er ___ far than milk? Sing
3. Oh, snow is whit - er ___ far than milk, Sing

nine - ty - nine and nine - ty, I'll take you off with ___
nine - ty - nine and nine - ty, And what is soft - er ___
nine - ty - nine and nine - ty, And down is soft - er ___

me to dwell, And you the weav - er - ing bon - ty.
far than silk? And you the weav - er - ing bon - ty.
far than silk, And me the weav - er - ing bon - ty.

4. Oh, what is louder than a horn?...
   And what is sharper than
   a thorn?...

5. Oh, thunder's louder than a horn,...
   And lightning's sharper than
   a thorn,...

6. Oh, what red fruit September
   grows?...
   And what thing round the whole
   world goes?...

7. The apple in September grows,...
   And air around the whole world
   goes,...

8. Oh, you have answered my questions
   well,...
   I'll take you off with me to dwell,...

Consolation

Shape Note Hymn
from *Southern Harmony*

1. Once more, my soul, the ___ ris - ing ___ day
2. Night un - to night His ___ name re - peats,
3. Dear God, let all my ___ hours be ___ thine

Sa - lutes thy wak - ing eyes; _____
The day re - news the sound, _____
Whilst I en - joy the light. _____

Once __ more, my __ voice, thy trib - ute ___ pay
Wide __ as the __ heav'n on which He __ sits
Then __ shall my __ sun in smiles de - cline

To Him that rules ___ the skies. _____
To turn the sea - sons round. _____
And bring a pleas - ant night. _____

80

This song is from an early hymn collection called the "Southern Harmony." In this book the songs were written with "shape notes." People who were not able to read the usual musical notation could find the tones of the melody by the shape of the notes.

CONSOLATION.

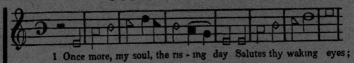

1 Once more, my soul, the ris - ing day Salutes thy waking eyes;

From William Walker's *Southern Harmony*, 1854.

Whippoorwill Round

Traditional

Gone to bed is the set - ting sun,

Night is com - ing and day is done, Whip-poor-

will, whip- poor- will, has just ___ be - gun.

81

Glendy Burke

Words and Music
by Stephen Foster

Stephen Foster was one of the first important American composers. Although
he lived in Pennsylvania, his music always has been associated with the South.
The music of "Glendy Burke" grew out of the banjo music Foster heard when
he roamed around the river wharfs as a young man.

1. The Glen-dy Burke is a might-y fast boat, With a might-y fast cap-tain
2. The Glen-dy Burke has a fun-ny old crew, And they sing the boat-man's

too;   He sits   up   there on the hur-ri-cane roof, And he
song; They burn the   pitch, and the pine _ knot too, For to

keeps his   eye   on the   crew.   I   can't stay   here, for they
shove the   boat   a -   long.   The smoke goes   up   and the

work too   hard; I'm bound to leave this town; I'll take my duds and
en-gine roars And the wheel goes round and round; So fare you well! for I'll

tote them on   my   back When the Glen-dy Burke comes down.
take a   lit-tle ride When the Glen-dy Burke comes down.

Refrain

Ho! for Loui - si - an - a! I'm bound to leave this town; I'll

take my duds and tote them on my back When the

Glen - dy Burke comes down.

Good Morning, Blues

Words and Music
by Huddie Ledbetter

The Negro sang as he worked; he sang as he worshiped. Sometimes he sang the "blues" in plaintive, wailing tones to express his loneliness.

1. Good morn - ing, blues; blues, how do you do?
2. Called yes - ter - day, here you come to - day.

Good morn - ing, blues; blues, how do you do?
Called yes - ter - day, here you come to - day.

I'm do - ing all right,— good morn - ing, how are you?
Your mouth's wide o - pen but you don't know what to say.

Follow the Drinkin' Gourd

Spiritual
Arranged by Paul Campbell

Read the words aloud and discuss their meaning. The drinking gourd is the North Star. Songs such as this one were used as signals among the slaves in the South to tell how to slip away and reach safety in the North.

Moderately

1. When the sun comes back and the first quail calls,—
2. Now the riv-er bank-'ll make— a might-y good road;— The
3. Now the riv - er ends— be-tween two hills;—

Fol - low____ the Drink - in' Gourd.— Then the
dead trees - 'll show you the way. And the
Fol - low ____ the Drink - in' Gourd.— And —

Old Man is a - wait - in' for to car - ry you to
left ___ foot, ___ peg - foot,— trav-el - in'___
there's an - oth - er riv - er on the oth - er ___

free - dom, Fol - low the Drink - in' Gourd.
on, Just you fol - low the Drink - in' Gourd.
side, Just you fol - low the Drink - in' Gourd.

New Words & New Music adaptation by Paul Campbell
TRO - Copyright 1951 Folkways Music Publishers, Inc.
New York, New York. Used by permission.

Refrain

Fol - low _____ the Drink - in' Gourd, _

Fol - low _____ the Drink - in' Gourd, _

For the Old Man is a - wait - in'

for to car - ry you to free - dom,

Fol - ow the Drink - in' Gourd.

Do you know what the meter signature ₵ means? To decide, listen to the recording and tap the beat. How does the rhythm move?

Notice this pattern.

It tells you to sing three quarter notes to one beat. How many quarter notes would we usually sing? The pattern of three is called a **triplet**.

Steal Away

Spiritual

This spiritual sometimes was used as a signal to Negroes who were planning to escape from slavery. The words "steal away" took on a second meaning.

Learn to sing this two-part arrangement. Notice that the melody is sometimes sung by high voices and sometimes by low voices. When you become familiar with the music, you may wish to improvise additional parts.

long _____ to stay here. 1. My Lord he calls
2. Green trees a - bend -

ain't got long to stay here.

1. My Lord he
2. Green trees, po'

me, _____ The trum-pet sounds_ with-
ing, _____ The trum-pet sounds_ with-

calls me by the thun-der, The trum - pet sounds with -
sin - ner stand a-tremb-ling, The trum - pet sounds with -

1.

in - a my soul. ...long _____ to stay here.
in - a my soul. ...long _____ to

in - a my soul. I ain't got long to stay here.
in - a my soul. I ain't got long to

2.

stay here, oh Lord, long _____ to stay here.

stay here, oh Lord _ I ain't got long to stay here.

Two Wings

Spiritual

Oh, Lord, I want two wings to veil my

Lord, I want to veil my

face; Oh, Lord, I want two wings to fly a-

face; Lord, I want to fly a-

way; Oh, Lord, I want two wings to veil my

way; Lord, I want to veil my

face, So the dev-il can't do me no harm._____

face, So the dev-il can't do me no harm.

Verse
Leader ... **Chorus**

My Lord, — did he come at the break — of day? No.
My Lord, — did he come in the heat — of noon? No.

Leader ... **Chorus**

My Lord, — did he come in the cool — of eve - ning? Yes!

D.C. al Fine

And he washed my sins a - way. _____

D.C. al Fine

And he washed my sins a - way.

From its beginning, Afro-American music has been a blending of many musical traditions. The spiritual, the work song, and the blues combined musical traditions brought from Africa with sounds of European music.

This blending of musical styles continues, as exhibited in modern gospel music heard in churches and on television and recordings.

Listen to "Two Wings," an old spiritual, sung in gospel style by James Cleveland and the Cleveland Singers. Discuss the differences between this arrangement and the one found in your book. Notice the instruments used in the accompaniment, the vocal style, and the type of harmonies used. Notice the question-answer dialogue between the soloist and chorus. What musical styles do you think are combined in this new music?

Somebody's Knockin' at Your Door

Spiritual
Arranged by Buryl A. Red

Some-bod - y's knock-ing at your door,_____

Some-bod - y's knock-ing at your

Some-bod - y's knock-ing at your door;_____

door,_____ Some-bod - y's knock-ing at your

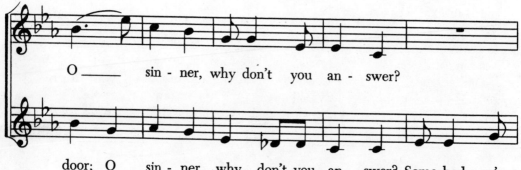

O_____ sin - ner, why don't you an - swer?

door; O sin - ner, why don't you an - swer? Some-bod - y's

Lonesome Valley

Spiritual
Arranged by Buryl A. Red

As people move to new regions, many influences affect their music. This lovely spiritual combines the traditional sounds of the English ballad with sounds from Africa. Listen again to "Farewell, My Own True Love" on page 78 and "Tina Singu" on page 20. Discuss characteristics you find in these songs that are also in the music of "Lonesome Valley."

1. Je-sus walked _____ this lone-some val-ley, _____ He had to
2. We must walk _____ this lone-some val-ley, _____ We have to

1. Je-sus walked this lone-some val-ley,
2. We must walk this lone-some val-ley,

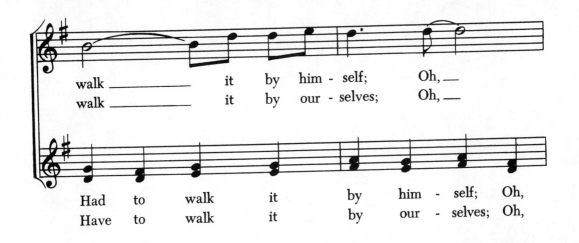

walk _____ it by him - self; Oh, —
walk _____ it by our - selves; Oh, —

Had to walk it by him - self; Oh,
Have to walk it by our - selves; Oh,

no-bod-y else ___ could walk it for Him, He had to
no-bod-y else ___ can walk it for us, We have to

No - bod-y could walk it for Him,
No - bod-y can walk it for us,

walk it by ___ him - self.
walk it by ___ our - selves.

Had to walk it by him - self.
Have to walk it by our - selves.

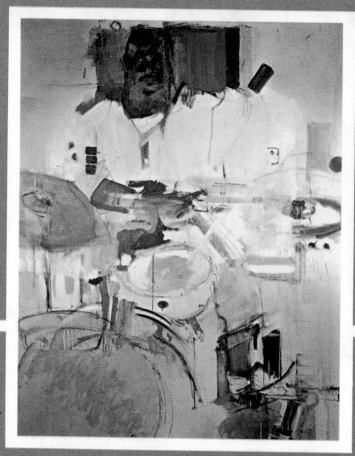

The Drummer
by Larry Rivers

When the Saints Go Marching In

New Words by Paul Campbell

In the early 1900's a new kind of music known as jazz began to emerge in New Orleans. Jazz is uniquely American. Musical ideas from Africa, Europe, and Latin America were blended together in the new sound.

Jazz began in the street bands of New Orleans. This early music is often called "Dixieland." "When the Saints Go Marching In" was a favorite tune of the street bands.

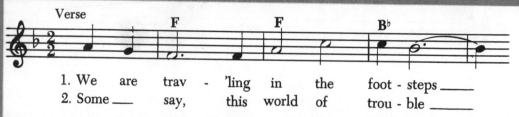

Verse

1. We are trav - 'ling in the foot - steps _____
2. Some _____ say, this world of trou - ble _____

94

of those who've gone be - fore, _____
is the on - ly _____ one we need, _____

But we'll all be re - u - nit - ed _____
But I'm wait - ing for that morn - ing _____

on a new and sun - lit shore. _____
when the new world is re - vealed. _____

Refrain

Oh, when the Saints _____ go march - ing in, _____

Oh, when the Saints go _____ march - ing in, _____

Oh, Lord, I _____ want to be in that num - ber _____

When the Saints go march - ing in. _____

DIXIELAND

Listen to a jazz combo playing in early Dixieland style.

The **rhythm section**—drums, banjo, and tuba—played an accompaniment such as this.

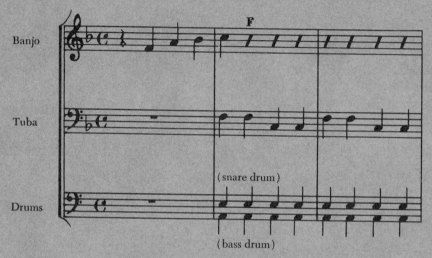

The melody was taken by the trumpet. The trumpet player would "decorate" the original melody in a variety of ways.

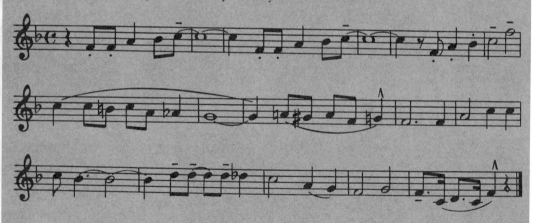

In a range below the melody, the trombone played the most important note of each chord.

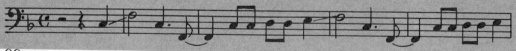

The clarinet played a busy part, filled with many notes, in harmony above the melody.

Now hear a complete jazz arrangement of "When the Saints Go Marching In."

Now listen to an arrangement of "Take the A Train," a more recent tune that is a favorite of jazz performers. It is played by Duke Ellington and his orchestra. What differences do you notice?

The last composition on your recording is played by the Ramsey Lewis Trio, a group which is popular today. The trio improvises on an old folk tune which you know as "The Riddle Song." Can you find the melody in the Lewis arrangement?

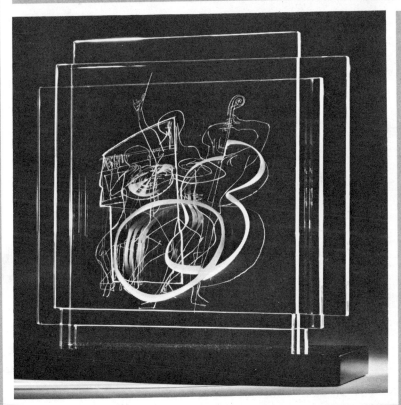

Jazz
Glass design by Jacob Landau
Engraved by Donald Pollard

Sweet Potatoes

Creole Folk Song
Adapted and Arranged
by Jean La Coste

Bamboula

by Louis Gottschalk

Bamboula is a vigorous Creole dance which was popular in New Orleans. It had its roots in Africa and the West Indies. People often danced it in the streets. "Sweet Potatoes" is based on the bamboula melody.

Louis Gottschalk, who lived in New Orleans during the middle 1800's, used this tune in a piano composition. Listen to his music. What changes did he make in the melody? How did he suggest the vigorous dance?

Prelude No. 2

by George Gershwin

A hundred years after Gottschalk was born, another American composer, George Gershwin, found many of his ideas in the music of the South and in jazz.

Listen to "Prelude No. 2." Compare it to "Bamboula." Do you hear any similarities between the two compositions?

Here is the beginning of Gershwin's composition. He did not use actual folk melodies, but his own melodies sound folk-like. Can you write words for the first part of the melody?

DANCE THE MINUET

As America grew and people gathered in the cities, they began to enjoy a musical life similar to the life they had left behind in Europe. They attended concerts and went to parties where they danced popular European dances, such as the minuet.

This minuet was used by Mozart in a ballroom scene in his opera, "Don Giovanni." Listen to the music and discover the design. Learn to dance the minuet. Does the style of the music help you know the style of dancing you should use?

Gai lon la, Gai le rosier

French Folk Song

1. Par der - rièr' chez ma tan - te, Lui ya' - t'un bois jo - li.
2. Le ros - si - gnol y chan - te Et le jour et la nuit.
3. Il chan - te pour les bel - les Qui n'ont pas de ma - ri.

Le ros - si - gnol y chan - te Et le jour et la nuit.
Il chan - te pour les bel - les Qui n'ont pas de ma - ri.
Il ne chan - te pas pour moi — Car j'en ai un jo - li.

Gai lon la, Gai le ro - sier, Du jo - li mois de mai. —

100

Acadian Songs and Dances

by Virgil Thomson

Virgil Thomson is a composer who used folk melodies in his music for orchestra. What other composers have you studied who drew from folk material for their music?

In this suite, "Acadian Songs and Dances," Thomson chose to use Louisiana folk music, the tunes of the Cajun river people. The Cajuns are descendants of French people who long ago moved to Louisiana from Acadia in Nova Scotia, Canada.

As you listen to three sections of the suite, decide whether you are hearing all of each melody, or only part of it. Do the melodies change each time you hear them, or are they repeated exactly?

Papa's Tune

Learn to sing this brief Cajun song before you listen to Thomson's music.

Not Far from My Home

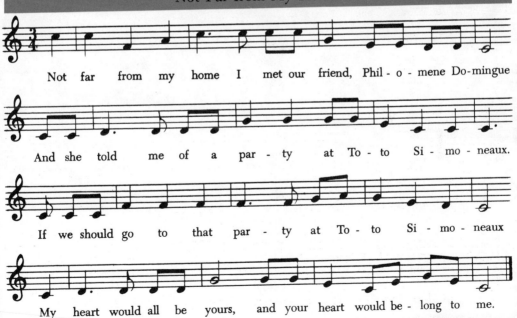

Not far from my home I met our friend, Phil-o-mene Do-mingue

And she told me of a par-ty at To-to Si-mo-neaux.

If we should go to that par-ty at To-to Si-mo-neaux

My heart would all be yours, and your heart would be-long to me.

101

As you sing the song, notice how personal it is; it was sung about specific people who lived in a specific place. Many Cajun songs are like that. Toto Simoneaux was a real person. It was said he had a very long beard, parted in two and tied at the back of his neck!

How many times is the melody repeated in "Papa's Tune"? How is it played differently the second time? What instrument does the sound of the orchestra suggest?

The Alligator and the 'Coon

Several Cajun melodies appear in "The Alligator and the 'Coon." Learn to sing the one that is heard most often.

The people of St. Martinville used to sing this song when they saw the Voorhies family on the way to the church of St. Martin. Judge Voorhies had fourteen children!

Who Is Passing By?

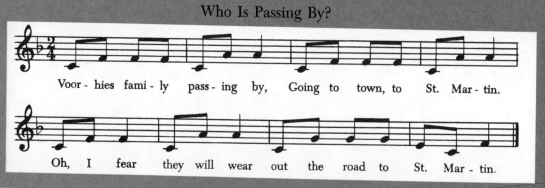

Voor - hies fami - ly pass - ing by, Going to town, to St. Mar - tin.

Oh, I fear they will wear out the road to St. Mar - tin.

The original words of this song were about a thief who was trying to steal Madame Baptiste's chickens. Sing the melody with "loo." Make up your own words.

Madame Baptiste

Does the same instrument always play the same melody? Identify the solo instruments you hear. What is unusual about the final chord which ends the movement?

Super-Sadness

Sad Song

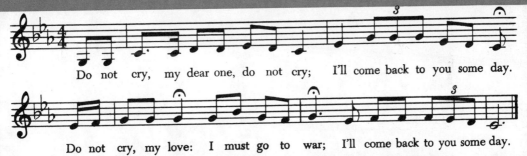

Do not cry, my dear one, do not cry; I'll come back to you some day.

Do not cry, my love: I must go to war; I'll come back to you some day.

What instruments does the composer use to strengthen the plaintive mood? Listen to the simple accompaniment. In this movement, the composer has used the folk melody exactly as in the original. The meaning of the words is reflected in his music.

Music of the Middle West

As people moved into the Middle West, their frontier life was accompanied by music, just as it had been in the East and South. Since there were few instruments and no theaters, people supplied their own music. They sang folk songs and accompanied themselves as they danced. They also created new songs to accompany their work, worship, and social life.

The Middle West, with its rich farm lands and forest, drew people from the Scandinavian countries and Western Europe. As cities such as Detroit and Chicago grew up around the Great Lakes, thousands of people from Russia, Poland, Czechoslovakia, and other Central European countries arrived. Each group brought its own songs and instrumental music.

As the years passed, the sound of hammers, machinery, and train whistles gave evidence of a growing industrial life in the Middle West. These changes were reflected in new music — songs of the railroad and of the assembly line.

Among the many people who migrated to the Middle West were fine composers, performers, and teachers. Factories began making musical instruments, and teachers of these instruments were in demand. Now that more people were living in cities, more types of music could be enjoyed. Concerts by symphony orchestras, bands, and operatic groups began to be a part of the sound of music in the Middle West as well as in other parts of the United States.

Music is still an important part of life in the Middle West. Most schools have marching and concert bands, orchestras, and choirs. People sing in church choirs, play in town bands, and gather in each other's homes to make music. Many people earn their living by playing in civic orchestras or in popular "combos." The tradition of making music for themselves has continued among midwestern people.

Shuckin' of the Corn

American Folk Song

1. I have a ship on the o - cean, ___
2. The wind blows cold in ___ Cai - ro, ___

All lined with sil - ver and gold. ___
The sun re - fus - es to shine. ___

Be - fore I'd see my true love suf - fer,
Be - fore I'd see my true love suf - fer,

That ship should be an - chored and sold. ___
I'd work all the sum - mer time. ___

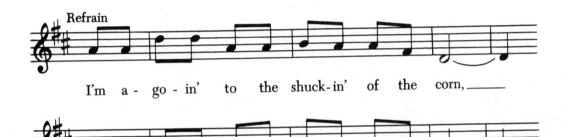

Refrain

I'm a - go - in' to the shuck - in' of the corn, ____

I'm a - go - in' to the shuck - in' of the corn, ____

A - shuck - in' of the corn, and a - blow - in' of the horn,

I'm a - go - in' to the shuck - in' of the corn. ____

Review the discussion on pages 32-33, and plan a harmonizing part for the refrain.

Add a rhythmic accompaniment.

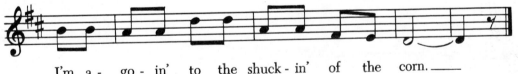

Clap Hands

Tap Feet

The Farmer Is the Man

Midwestern Folk Song

Study the design of this song. Why will it be easy to learn?

Play a steady beat in fours on a wood block in a moderate **tempo**. Chant the words in rhythm.

1. When the farm-er comes to town,With his wag-on bro-ken down,Oh, the
2. The — doc-tor hangs a-round While the black-smith heats his iron,Oh, the

farm - er is the man who feeds them all! If you'll
farm - er is the man who feeds them all! The —

on - ly look and see, I — think you will a-gree That the
preach-er and the cook Go — stroll-ing by the brook, And the

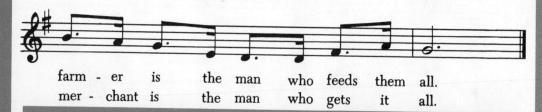

farm - er is the man who feeds them all.
mer - chant is the man who gets it all.

Play 1 3 5 on the bells. Can you sing the melody immediately with words? If you have problems, practice singing with numbers.

Red River Valley

American Folk Song

This song was originally known as "In the Bright Mohawk Valley." The valley is in the eastern part of the United States. As the pioneers carried the song westward, the words were changed to fit the new region. Find the Red River on a map of the United States.

1. From this val - ley, they say, you are go - ing, _____
Refrain: *Come and sit by my side if you love me,* _____

We will miss your bright eyes and sweet smile,
Do not has - ten to bid me a - dieu,

For they say you are tak - ing the sun - shine
But re - mem - ber the Red Riv - er Val - ley

That bright - ens our path - way a - while. _____
And the girl that has loved you so true. _____

2. Won't you think of the valley you're leaving?
Oh, how lonely, how sad it will be.
Oh, think of the fond heart you're breaking,
And the grief you are giving to me.
Refrain

PLAY-PARTY TIME

The settlers worked hard clearing land, planting crops, building homes. When the work was done, they played! On Saturday nights everyone would gather at the schoolhouse for a "play-party." All of them, old and young, joined in the games. People who were too tired to dance sat around the edge of the room and sang or kept time with feet and hands.

The settlers had brought their dances with them from Scotland, England, Ireland, and Germany. In those countries the dances were usually accompanied by instrumental music. In the frontier settlements there were few instruments, so the people sang as they danced. Sometimes they set words to fiddle tunes, or made up new dance words to familiar melodies.

Some of the dances these people enjoyed were line dances. This dance, called "Your Best Liking," is done to the tune of "Ten Little Indians." The words tell you the dance patterns.

1. Meeting halfway with your best liking,
   Meeting halfway with your best liking,
   Meeting halfway with your best liking,
   For she is your darling.

2. Right hand round, etc.

3. Left hand round, etc.

4. Both hands round, etc.

5. Do-si-do, etc.

6. Turn right and left, etc.

7. All run away, etc.

1. Gents to the center, Skip to my Lou;
   Gents to the center, Skip to my Lou;
   Gents to the center, Skip to my Lou;
   Skip to my Lou, my darling!

2. Ladies to the center, etc.

3. Bow to your partner, etc.

4. Now to your opposite, etc.

5. Promenade all and, etc.

6. Lost my lover, what shall I do?

7. I found another one, just as true.

Other dances the pioneers enjoyed were circle dances. Dancers formed a single circle, facing the center of the ring. Girls were on the right of their partners. The dance above is done to the tune of "Skip to My Lou."

Square dances were the most popular of all. Four couples made up a square, with the girl on her partner's right. A "caller" called out the patterns for the dancers to follow. Some of the dances had "singing calls." The "singing square" below is done to the tune of "Red River Valley."

1. Now, the first couple leads down the valley,
       (dance with second couple)
   Circle left, then you circle to the right
   Now you swing that girl in the valley
   And you swing your own Red River Gal.
2. Now you lead right on down the valley, etc.
       (dance with couple no. 3)
3. Now you lead right on down the valley, etc.
       (dance with couple no. 4)
4. Now it's allemande left to your corner
   And a right hand to your own
   And when you meet your partner
   Then you promenade her on home.

Boy Fishing
by Winslow Homer

Father of Waters
and Huckleberry Finn

from *Mississippi Suite*

by Ferde Grofé

FATHER OF WATERS

The great Mississippi River cuts a mighty path through the center of the United States. To millions of people who have lived and worked along its shores, it is indeed, the "Father of Waters." This is the title Ferde Grofé gave one of the **movements** of his **suite**.

Listen to the music. How does the composer let you know he is describing a mighty river? Look at the main theme as you listen.

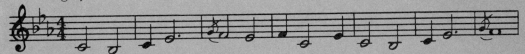

The composer depends on your knowledge of history of the river to understand his musical description. What does the introduction suggest? At one point the music describes a group of people who once lived along the river. How does the music help you know who they are?

HUCKLEBERRY FINN

In this section Grofé gives a musical description of a character created by the famous American writer, Mark Twain. Twain wrote many tales of life along the Mississippi.

Listen to the music. What does it tell you about Huckleberry Finn? Does he have the same feeling all the way through the music?

The *Mississippi Suite* is **program music**. In music of this type the composer describes something very definite. He wants you to imagine a place, a person, a story, or a particular mood as you listen. In other compositions the composer is interested in writing music that deals only with musical ideas. He wants you to listen for the different ways he has combined the musical elements.

What other program music have you studied this year? What compositions have you heard that are not program music?

Bound for the Promised Land

American Folk Hymn

1. On Jor - dan's storm - y banks I stand And
2. There gen-er-ous fruits that nev - er fail On

cast a wish - ful eye; To ___ Ca - naan's fair and
trees im - mor - tal grow; There ___ rocks and ___ hills and

hap - py land Where ___ my pos - ses - sions lie.
brooks and vales With ___ milk and ___ hon - ey flow.

Refrain

I am bound for the prom - ised land, _____ I'm

bound for the prom - ised land; Oh, ___ who will ___ come and

go with me, I am bound for the prom - ised land.

No Wood-Fire and No Coal-Flame

German Folk Song
English Translation
by Babette Deutsch

As you learn this German folk song and other songs from foreign countries on the following pages, locate, on a map, the countries represented by each song. People from these countries helped to settle the Middle West.

Someone may play the lower part on the recorder or other melody instrument.

1. No wood-fire and no coal-flame So burning-ly glows As love that is hidden, And that no-bod-y knows, And that no-bod-y knows.
2. In my heart pray set a mir-ror And there-in you'll see My faith and my wor-ship Are on-ly for thee, Are on-ly for thee!

Over the Meadow

Czechoslovakian Folk Melody
Words by Beth Landis
Arranged by Kurt Miller

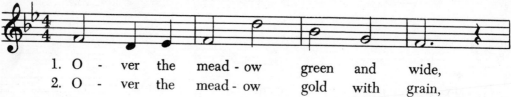

1. O - ver the mead - ow green and wide,
2. O - ver the mead - ow gold with grain,

Sun - light is stream - ing, sun - light is stream - ing,
Har - vest is sun - ning, har - vest is sun - ning,

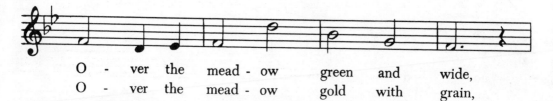

O - ver the mead - ow green and wide,
O - ver the mead - ow gold with grain,

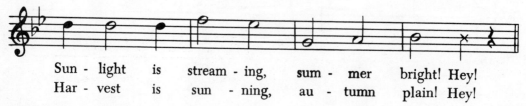

Sun - light is stream - ing, sum - mer bright! Hey!
Har - vest is sun - ning, au - tumn plain! Hey!

Refrain

Wind - ing, Shin - ing,

(Melody)

Wind - ing down moun-tain-side, Shin - ing small riv - ers glide,

Join - ing riv - er wide,— Splash-ing spar-kling sand;

Join - ing the riv - er wide, Splash-ing the spar-kling sand,—

Wind - ing, Shin - ing,

Wind - ing down moun-tain-side, Shin - ing small riv - ers glide,

Join - ing riv - er wide,— Pride — of our land! Hey!

Join - ing the riv - er wide, Pride of our land! Hey!

Song of the Sea

Russian Folk Song
English words by William S. Haynie

On what scale is the song based? Learn to sing the song in harmony. You will sing these intervals.

sixth   fifth   fourth   third   second   unison

Divide into two groups and sing each interval. Listen to the sound. Find the intervals in the song.

I   will   sing   a - bout   my   lov - er   who   has

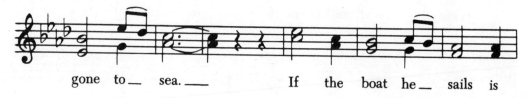

gone to __ sea. __   If   the   boat   he __   sails   is

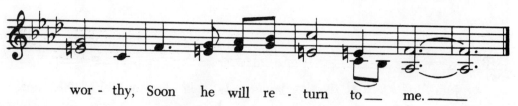

wor - thy, Soon   he   will   re - turn   to __   me. ____

118

Forest Gypsy

Polish Folk Melody
Translation by Beth Landis

Learn to sing this song by reading the notes. When you know the melody, add a harmonizing part to the refrain. Sing in thirds and sixths.

1. Deep in the for - est, gay gyp - sy cho - rus,
2. No land to hold him, no law to mold him,
3. Warm camp - fires burn - ing, beck - on the yearn - ing,

Bright glow - ing camp - fire leap - ing be - fore us.
Light - heart - ed gyp - sy, free days en - fold him.
Wel - come the wan - der - er home - ward re - turn - ing.

Refrain

Boom tra - le la - le, boom tra - le la - le,

boom tra - le la - le oo, ha ha,

Boom tra - le la - le, boom tra - le la - le oo, ha ha, hee.

119

Morning Comes Early

Slovak Folk Song
Words Adapted

1. Morn - ing comes ear - ly, the dew so bright.
2. Lis - ten, my com - rade: when work seems long,

Come with me, lad - die, in day's first light.
Light - en each mo - ment with mer - ry song.

Dawn o - ver - takes me, morn - ing a - wakes me,
Wel - come to - mor - row, wait not for sor - row,

To the green mead - ows the herd I lead.
Mu - sic and laugh - ter are all we need!

The village orchestras in Czechoslovakia often included a violin, clarinet, trumpet, and "hurdy-gurdy," a kind of small organ. Members of the class who are studying instruments may wish to learn to play this song. One person may play the melody while another person plays this accompaniment.

The Praties They Grow Small

Irish Folk Song

1. Oh, the pra - ties they grow small o - ver here, o - ver here, Oh, the pra - ties they grow small, and we dig them in the fall, And we eat them coats and all o - ver here, o - ver here.

2. Oh, I wish that we were geese, night and morn, night and morn, Oh, I wish that we were geese, for they fly and take their ease, And they live and die in peace eat - in' corn, eat - in' corn.

3. Oh, we're hop - ing for the day o - ver here, o - ver here, Oh, we're hop - ing for the day when to oth - ers we can say, This is home and here we'll stay, o - ver here, o - ver here.

Notice the D♯ in measure one. This is called an **accidental** because the note is not part of the scale on which the song is based.

Sing these two patterns. Discuss the differences.

SONGS OF THE RAILROAD

The songs of the railroad describe an exciting period in the history of our country. Listen to "The Fireball Mail," a modern railroad song which catches the flavor of the pounding wheels of the locomotive. Contrast this with the song "Nine Hundred Miles" which expresses the loneliness of a traveller.

In the early days, Americans moved by foot, on horseback, in wagons, boats, and barges. As better machinery, building materials, and fuels were developed, the first railroads were begun. Listen to "Paddy Works on the Railway," a song sung by Irish workers as they heaped up the gravel beds, lifted the ties into place, and spiked down rails on lines that led from New York across the Middle West.

The railroad gangs in the South sang songs to help them keep up their grueling work for long hours under the hot sun. An expert worker set the pace with exactly the right tempo. These song leaders had a different song for each part of their job.

For example, after the rails were spiked down, they had to be straightened so that they were the same distance apart. This job was called "tie shuffling." The foreman called his instructions to the song leader who would sing: "All I hate about linin' track, these old bars about to break my back."

With the chorus, the man heaved against the bars, once to every line:
   "Ho boys, can't you line 'em?"

Next, the men packed gravel around the ties to hold the rails in line under the force of the speeding train. The irregular rhythm of the "Tie-Tamping Song" matched the rhythm of the tampers.

The toughest job on the railroad, tunnel building, produced the greatest of our railroad heroes, John Henry. John Henry was a steel driller. He hammered holes into the hard rock so that dynamite could be placed to blast the mountain.

Then one day, the newly-invented steam drill arrived. The engineer in charge posed a contest between John Henry and the steam drill. The story goes that John Henry beat the steam drill, but that he hammered so hard and so fast that he broke his heart and died. His ballad lives as one of our greatest American folk songs.

WESTWARD HO! A MIME.

Develop a pantomime that helps express the drama of building railroads across our country.

Some ideas that might be included in your pantomime are:

> Work in twos and hammer the
> spikes into the rails to the
> rhythm of "Fireball Mail."
> One heavy hammer falls as the
> other one rises . . .

>> Four or six people are needed to heave the heavy
>> ties in place as the leader sings the "Tie-Shuffling
>> Song."

Use different rhythms to tamp the gravel around the ties as the singer urges, "do it—you can do it, you can . . ."

You've been building a great railroad
in the wilderness. Now, back to camp.
The day's work is over, and it's time
to relax. You sing and even make up
a swaggering dance . . . hands in your
pockets and walk in a circle:

In eighteen hundred and forty one
(*walk in swaggering style in a circle*)

I put me corduroy britches on
(*one catch step, continue walking in circle*)

I put me corduroy britches on
(*one catch step, turn walk to center of
circle*)

To work upon the railway.
(*step backwards
out of circle*)

Fil-i-mee-oo-re-i-re-ay
(*pantomime swinging heavy sledge ham-
mer on accented syllables*)

Fil-i-mee-oo-re-i-re-ay

Fil-i-mee-oo-re-i-re-ay

To work upon the railway.
(*catch step, pivot in circle*)

Repeat this movement with each new
verse of the song.

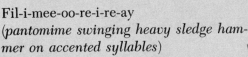

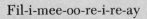

Listen to other work songs. Can you make up your own movement games
which reflect the heavy rhythmic sounds of hammers and massive movements
involved in the work?

Han Skal Leve

Danish Folk Song

Han skal le - ve, han skal le - ve,

han skal le - ve højt, hur - rah!

Han skal le - ve, han skal le - ve,

Fine

han skal le - ve højt, hur - rah!

Hur - ra, hur - ra, hur - ra, hur - ra, hur - ra,

Hur - ra, hur - ra, hur - ra, hur - ra, hur - ra!

126

Han skal le - ve, han skal le - ve,

han skal le - ve højt, hur - rah!

Bra - vo, bra - vo, bra - vo, bra - vis - si - mo,

bra - vo, bra - vo, bra - vis - si - mo;

Bra - vo, bra - vis - si - mo, bra - vo, bra - vis - si - mo,

D.C. al Fine

bra - vo, bra - vo, bra - vis - si - mo!

The Lord's My Shepherd

Scottish Hymn Tune
Paraphrase of Psalm 23
by James L. Bain

The melody for this beautiful hymn comes from Scotland. Some members of the class may sing the descant. Notice that the descant is made up of scale patterns and patterns with tones from the I chord.

Ah, _____ Ah, _____

(Melody)

1. The Lord's my shep - herd; I'll not want. He makes me down to
2. My soul he doth re - store a - gain and me to walk doth
3. And though I pass through shad-owed vale, yet will I fear no

_____ Ah, _____ Ah, _____

lie   In pas - tures green. He lead - eth me the
make   With - in the paths of bless - ed - ness e'en
ill,   For thou art with me, and thy rod and

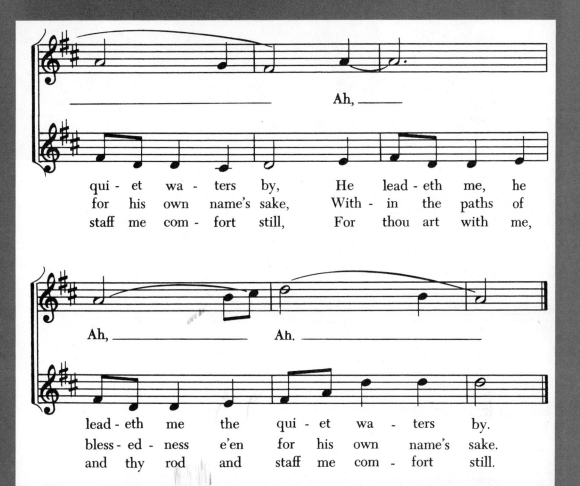

qui - et wa - ters by, He lead - eth me, he
for his own name's sake, With - in the paths of
staff me com - fort still, For thou art with me,

Ah, _____ _____

Ah, _____ Ah. _____

lead - eth me the qui - et wa - ters by.
bless - ed - ness e'en for his own name's sake.
and thy rod and staff me com - fort still.

4. My table thou hast furnished in presence of my foes.
My head with oil thou dost anoint, and my cup overflows,
My head with oil thou dost anoint, and my cup overflows.

5. Goodness and mercy all my days will surely follow me,
And in my Father's heart alway my dwelling place shall be,
And in my Father's heart alway my dwelling place shall be.

Over My Head

Spiritual
Arranged by Buryl A. Red

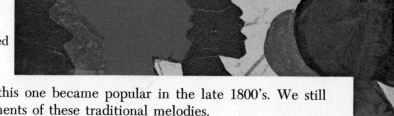

Gospel songs such as this one became popular in the late 1800's. We still enjoy singing arrangements of these traditional melodies.

O - ver my head _____

O - ver my

air. _____

_____ I hear mu - sic in the air, in the air. ___ There

head I hear mu - sic in the air, in the air. ___

where. _____

must be a God some - where, some - where.

If I Had a Hammer

Words and Music
by Lee Hays and Pete Seeger

This modern folk song has many of the characteristics of songs first sung during an earlier time. Compare it with the melodies you heard in "Songs of the Railroad."

Locate syncopated patterns. As one person taps the beat, chant the words in rhythm.

On what scale is this song based? Find a melody pattern which includes an **accidental**. What does it tell you to do?

1. If I had a ham-mer,— I'd ham-mer in the
   bell,———— I'd ring it in the
   song,———— I'd sing it in the
   ham-mer,— And I've— got a

   morn-ing,— I'd ham-mer in the eve-ning,—
   morn-ing,— I'd ring it in the eve-ning,—
   morn-ing,— I'd sing it in the eve-ning,—
   bell,———— And I've— got a song,————

132

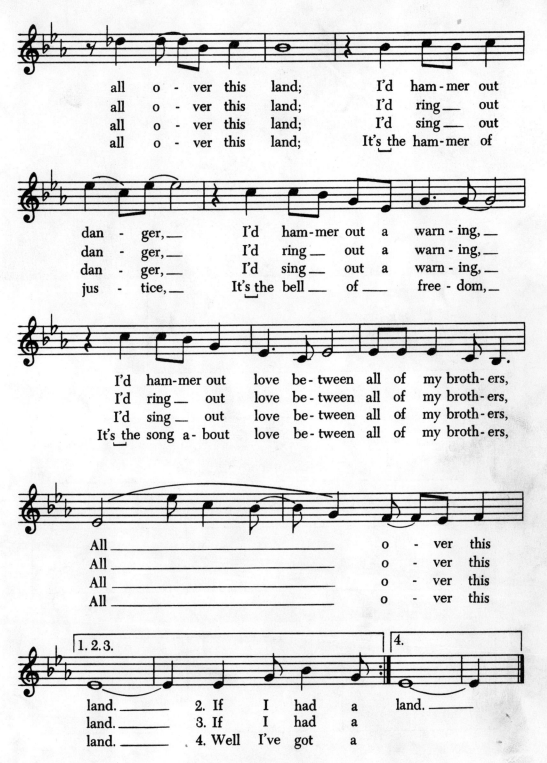

all o - ver this land;   I'd ham-mer out
all o - ver this land;   I'd ring___ out
all o - ver this land;   I'd sing___ out
all o - ver this land;   It's the ham-mer of

dan - ger,___   I'd ham-mer out a warn - ing,___
dan - ger,___   I'd ring___ out a warn - ing,___
dan - ger,___   I'd sing___ out a warn - ing,___
jus - tice,___   It's the bell___ of ___ free - dom,___

I'd ham-mer out love be - tween all of my broth - ers,
I'd ring___ out love be - tween all of my broth - ers,
I'd sing___ out love be - tween all of my broth - ers,
It's the song a - bout love be - tween all of my broth - ers,

All _____ o - ver this
All _____ o - ver this
All _____ o - ver this
All _____ o - ver this

1. 2. 3.

land. _____ 2. If I had a
land. _____ 3. If I had a
land. _____ 4. Well I've got a

4.

land. _____

Classical Symphony, Opus 25

by Serge Prokofiev

Listen to a composition made up of four separate parts, or **movements**.

The entire composition is described as a **symphony**. After you have listened to all of the movements, make up your own definition for this word.

As you listen to each movement, follow the chart. Some parts of the chart contain questions. Can you answer them?

MOVEMENT I   **Allegro = ?**

Theme 1: instruments? Theme 2: woodwinds and strings Theme 3: violins	new themes? or old themes?	which themes?

MOVEMENT II   **Larghetto = ?**

introduction	high theme: strings	new themes? or old themes?	which themes?	coda

MOVEMENT III   **A gavotte** is a ?

Gavotte phrases a b c b c	Trio phrases?	?

MOVEMENT IV   **Molto vivace = ?**

Theme 1 Theme 2: full orchestra Theme 3: flutes	exactly the same?	Theme 3: clarinet others?	Theme 1: strings Theme 2 Theme 3

An Event for Three Performers & a Conductor

Each performer must

- play one melodic and one non-pitched instrument or use vocal and body sounds
- begin at the point designated for him in the score
- decide how he will interpret the symbols in each box
- determine his own route through the score by following the arrows.

The conductor signals to tell the performers when to

- begin playing
- move to a new box
- end the composition.

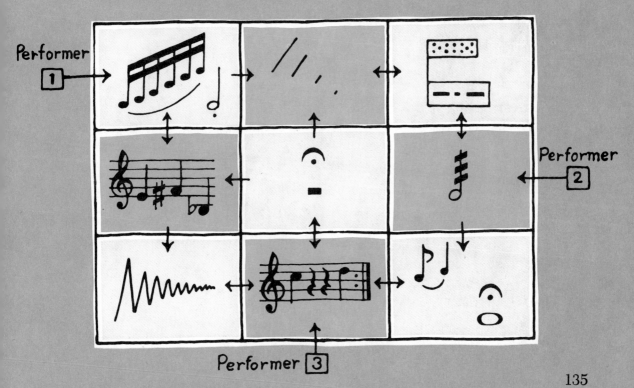

Music of the Far West

The movement West was one of the great adventures of the world. People from all walks of life joined in migration. They found broad prairies, grazing lands, rugged mountains, fertile valleys, barren deserts, and thick forests. They found people who were there before them — Indians, traders, and missionaries. When they reached New Mexico and California, they found Spanish-speaking people who had come from Spain and Mexico.

The great adventure was filled with hardship and sorrow, happiness and humor. The daily events were recorded in music. The folk songs of the westward expansion are an interesting record of the thoughts and feelings of the people who participated in it.

Some of the people who settled the West were from other nations. Europeans came to work the land, as they had done in the East and in the Middle West. Later, Asian people traveled across the Pacific to make homes along the West Coast or to help build railroads. They joined the groups already there and soon the West, like other regions of the country, was hearing music from many lands.

Today many musical events and accomplishments take place in the great cities of the West. Film music, rock performers, and jazz groups are notable. Great performers of the world are heard in opera, oratorio, and symphony. Fine western composers are at work writing music. The great American adventure of moving from one place to another never has stopped. People continue to move west, and musical life there continues to grow richer.

So Long

Words and Music
by Woody Guthrie

Years of drought, wind, and dust drove many farmers out of Oklahoma, Kansas, and eastern Colorado in the 1930's. This song by Woody Guthrie describes the feelings of those people. Guthrie's songs, like those of Stephen Foster, resemble folk songs. Discuss the words and melody of the song. Why does this song seem like a folk song?

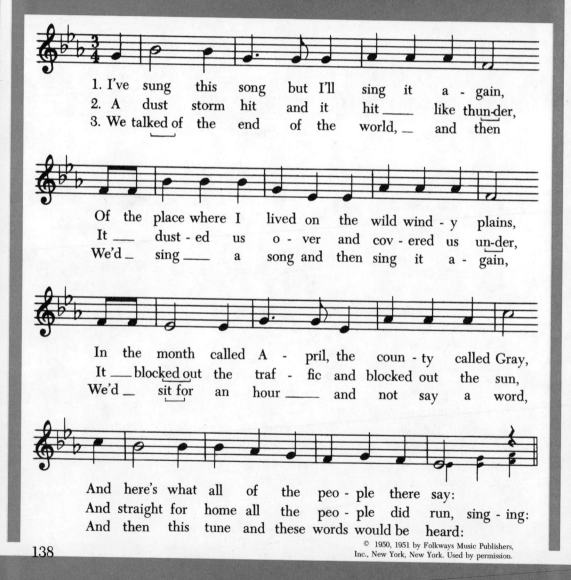

1. I've sung this song but I'll sing it a - gain,
2. A dust storm hit and it hit ____ like thun-der,
3. We talked of the end of the world, __ and then

Of the place where I lived on the wild wind - y plains,
It ___ dust - ed us o - ver and cov - ered us un-der,
We'd _ sing ____ a song and then sing it a - gain,

In the month called A - pril, the coun - ty called Gray,
It ___ blocked out the traf - fic and blocked out the sun,
We'd _ sit for an hour ____ and not say a word,

And here's what all of the peo - ple there say:
And straight for home all the peo - ple did run, sing - ing:
And then this tune and these words would be heard:

Refrain

"So long, it's been good to know you,

So long, it's been good to know you,

So long, it's been good to know you,

This dust - y old dust is a - get - ting my home,

I've got to be mov - ing a - long."_____

Dogie Song

Cowboy Song

Study the design. How many **sections** do you find? How many **phrases**? How many **motives** are included in each phrase? Do you find motives that are exactly the same? that are slightly altered?

Look at the key signature; study the notes of the song. Determine home tone. Sing 5 (low) 1 3 5 3 1. How much of the melody can you sing with words? Listen to the recording to correct any errors you may have made.

1. As   I   was a - walk - ing   one   morn - ing for pleas - ure,
2. It's whoop - ing and yell - ing and   driv - ing the do - gies,

I   spied   a cow - punch - er   all   rid - ing a - long;
And   oh,   how I   wish you would on - ly   go   on;

His   hat was throwed back and his   spurs was a - jin - gling,
It's whoop - ing and punch - ing, go   on,   lit - tle do - gies,

And   as   he ap - proached he   was   sing - ing this   song:
You   know   that Wy - o - ming will   be   your new   home.

Whoop-ee ti yi yo, ____ git a-long, lit-tle do-gies,

It's your mis-for-tune and none of my own,

Whoop-ee ti yi yo, ____ git a-long, lit-tle do-gies,

You know that Wy-o-ming will be your new home.

The Colorado Trail

Cowboy Song
Arranged by Kurt Miller

oo _____

oo _____

(Melody)

Eyes like the morn- ing star, Cheek like a rose,

oo _____

oo _____

Lau - ra was a pret- ty girl, ev - ery- bod - y knows.

oo _____

oo _____

Weep, all ye lit - tle rains, Wail, winds,— wail,

142

'Long the Col - o - ra - do Trail. __

All a - long, a - long, a - long the Col - o - ra - do Trail. __

Oklahoma!

by Richard Rodgers
and Oscar Hammerstein II

Many of the musical forms used by American composers were first developed by composers of Europe. One form which is truly American, however, is the **musical comedy**. In a musical comedy, words, music, and dance are combined to dramatize a story. There is dialogue as in a play. There are also songs and dances to help set the mood of a scene, describe the feelings of the characters, or tell part of the story.

The musical comedy *Oklahoma!* by Rodgers and Hammerstein is a tale of life in the Oklahoma territory just before it became a state. *Oklahoma!* is the story of a cowboy and his girl. The show opens with Curly, the hero, singing "Oh, What a Beautiful Morning." He is on his way to ask his girl, Laurey, to go to the box-social that evening. Later he describes for Laurey the surrey which he has rented to drive her to the party. When he finishes singing "The Surrey with the Fringe on Top," he admits that his description was mostly imagination!

At the dance, Curly asks Laurey to marry him. Later, at the wedding, the guests sing about their brand-new state, "Oklahoma!"

Listen to these three songs from the musical comedy. Notice how the music for each song supports the mood of the words. Discuss the differences in melodic contour and rhythmic movement of each. How do the different combinations of instruments support the mood of each song? How does the singers' style help to create the appropriate feeling in each song?

143

Deep in the Heart of Texas

Music by Don Swander
Words by June Hershey

Tex - as! _____ Re - minds me of the one I love, Deep in the heart of Tex - as! _____

The Texas Star

Western Square Dance

"The Texas Star" is one of the most popular American square dances. It is danced to a "patter call" which varies somewhat with each caller. Listen to the music. Discover the aabb design. Each theme is eight measures long.

Counting two beats to a measure, the first two dance figures in each verse take eight measures to complete. The third figure lasts for sixteen measures.

Take turns being the caller. Here are some calls you can use.

Introduction: All jump up, and when you come down
Swing your partner round and around
And promenade, boys, promenade!...

Dance: Ladies to the center and back to the bar
Gents to the center for the Texas Star
With the right hand in...

Back with the left and don't get lost...
Meet your partner, pass her by
Take the next one on the fly

Gents swing out and ladies in
Form that Texas Star again...
Ladies out, gents swing in

Make that star go round again
Break that star and give her a swing
Promenade this one round the ring

Promenade!...
Back to your place...
Here we go...

Jingle, Jangle, Jingle

Music by Joseph J. Lilley
Words by Frank Loesser

You know many cowboy songs which are folk songs. This cowboy song was composed by a popular song writer of the twentieth century.

How will the rhythm move? If you are not sure what this meter signature means, listen to the recording and tap the beat. What note will sound with the beat?

Learn to sing the song in harmony. Most of the harmony is created by **imitation**. Study the two parts to decide what this means. What kind of harmony do you find in the second phrase of the verse?

And they sing, "Oh, ain't you glad you're sin - gle!" ____

mer - ri - ly a - long. ____ And they sing, "Oh, ain't you

Fine

And that song ain't so ver - y far from wrong. ____

Fine

glad you're sin - gle!" ____ Sing that song. ____

Verse

1. Oh, Sal - ly Jane, ____ Oh, Sal - ly Jane, ____
2. Oh, Bes - sie Lou, ____ Oh, Bes - sie Lou, ____

Oh, Sal - ly Jane, Oh, Sal - ly Jane,
Oh, Bes - sie Lou, Oh Bes - sie Lou,

D.C. al Fine

Though I'd love to stay for - ev - er, This is why I can't re - main,
Though we'd done a heap of dream - in', This is why it won't come true,

147

Hoe-Down

from *Rodeo*

by Aaron Copland

Listen to "Hoe-Down," and enjoy the musical description of a Saturday night dance in the West. What is described in the introductory section of the composition? What seems to be described in the rhythmic **interlude** section? What is the overall design of the composition?

Listen again and follow the quick themes. For the A theme, the composer used a traditional square-dance tune. What instrument do the violins of the orchestra imitate? Describe the ways part two of the A theme is played.

Aaron Copland is a distinguished American composer who excels in writing music for the ballet. "Hoe-Down" is part of a ballet called *Rodeo* which tells the story in music and dance of a day of rodeo activities. Agnes de Mille was **choreographer** for the ballet when it was performed for the first time in 1942 at the Metropolitan Opera House in New York.

Plan your own class dance for "Hoe-Down." Count the measures in each section of the music. Use square-dance steps you know and any other movements you think suitable. Decide on the kind of movement you will use for each section of the music. Work on that movement until it matches the rhythm and phrasing of the music. Dance your dance with the entire composition.

148

Loneliness Song

Navaho Indian Song
Adapted and Arranged
by Louis W. Ballard

As ____ I walk,
She ____ na' sha,

as ____ I walk,
she ____ na' sha,

As ____ I
She ____ na'

walk, O may my path be beau-ti - ful for me,
sha, B' keh huh zho-la he - yah heyn' neh' yuh.

Or I'm a - lone in my lone - li - ness. ____
Ah' ah' luh, ah' ah' luh koh' nuh sha. ____

Raccoon Song

Shawnee Indian Stomp-Dance Melody
Adapted and Arranged
by Louis W. Ballard

This dance originated with the Seminole and Creek Indians of Florida. Compare the song with the one on page 149, sung by Navaho Indians of the Southwest.

Lah - tee tahk - wah, ___

H'yo - nah - weh,

H'yo - o wah - lee h'yo lee. ___

H'yo - nah - weh.

151

Come, Come, Ye Saints

"All Is Well"
Adapted from J. T. White
The Sacred Harp, 1844
Words by William Clayton

The Mormons, a religious group, made the long trip west from Illinois to Utah. They suffered the hardships of travel in covered wagons. The words of this song tell of the great faith of these pioneers.

1. Come, come, ye saints, no toil nor la - bor fear,
2. We'll find the place which God for us pre- pared

But with joy wend our way.
Far a - way in the West,

Though hard to you this jour - ney may ap - pear,
Where none shall come to hurt or make a - fraid;

Grace shall be as your day.
There the saints will be blessed.

'Tis ___ bet - ter far ___ for us to strive, ___
We'll ___ make the air ___ with mu - sic ring, ___

Our use - less cares _____ from us to drive;
Shout prais - es to _____ our God and King;

Do this, and joy your hearts will swell,
A - bove the rest these words we'll tell,

All is well! all is well!
All is well! all is well!

Wanderin'

American Folk Song

1. I've been work - in' in the cit - y, I've been work - in' on the farm,
2. Oh, the blue sky up a - bove me, and the green grass on the ground;

But all I've got to show for it is mus - cle in my arm,
Been look - in' round for man - y things that I have nev - er found,

And it looks like I'm nev - er gon - na cease my wan - der - in'.

The Owlet

Mexican Folk Song
English Words Adapted

Different versions of this Spanish lullaby are sung by Spanish-Americans in the Southwest. Learn to sing this two-part arrangement.

Andantino

Te - co - lo - te,   Lit - tle   owl - et,_____

ti - ny   bird   of   the   ear - ly   morn,_____

Won't   you   lend   to   me   your   wing - lets_____

so   that   I   may   go   to   my   love?_____

154

Won't you lend me your lit - tle wing - lets, _____

won't you lend me your lit - tle wing - lets, _____

won't you lend me your lit - tle wing - lets _____

so that I may go to my love?

Te - cu - ru - cú y cú y cú,

te - cu - ru - cú y cú y cú.

Po - bre - ci - to te - co lo - te.

You are too tired _ to cry now. Te - cu - ru - cry. _____

El barco chiquitito

Le petit navire

The Little Ship

Traditional Folk Song

The first verse of this song is printed for you in Spanish, French, and English. Folk songs often cross borders and are adapted by people who speak different languages. Each group alters the song, and it is often impossible to tell where the song originated.

Ha - bí - a un bar - co chi - qui - ti - to, ha - bí - a un
Il é - tait un pe - tit na - vi - re, il é - tait
1. Oh, there was once a lit - tle ship,____ oh, there was

bar - co chi - qui - ti - to, que no sa -
un pe - tit na - vi - re, qui n'a - vait
once a lit - tle ship,____ And it had

bí - bí - bí - a na - ve - gar, que no sa bí - bí -
ja - ja - ja - mais na - vi - gué, qui n'a - vait ja - ja -
ne - ne - nev - er made a trip, and it had ne - ne -

bí - a na - ve - gar. O - é, o - é.____ boy.____
ja - mais na - vi - gué. O - hé, o - hé.____
nev - er made a trip. O ay, o ay.____

156

Versions about the little ship and the unlucky sailor boy can be found in France and Spain as well as in Canada and Latin America. Why do you suppose the song traveled so far?

2. It sailed around through waters cold,
   'Till no more foo-foo-food was in the hold.

3. And then the men the straws did deal,
   To see just who-who-who would make their meal.

4. The shortest straw the youngest drew,
   So he was de-de-destined to be stew.

5. Meanwhile the boy climbed up the mast,
   Hoping a shi-shi-ship would soon come past.

6. But not a thing was there to see,
   And so he fear-fear-feared they'd soon eat he.

7. And, as he prayed, fish by the peck
   Suddenly la-la-landed on the deck.

8. They ate the fish with shouts of joy
   And did not ea-ea-eat the cabin boy.

MUSIC OF MEXICO AND SPAIN

Listen to two Mexican dances. What helps you know that this music is Mexican?

The first dance, "Jarabe Tapatio," is played by a **mariachi** band. These bands originally included a guitar, a violin, and a trumpet or clarinet. What instruments do you hear?

There are nine different themes and four changes of meter in "Jarabe Tapatio" or "Hat Dance." Can you hear them?

The second dance is called "La Raspa" or "The File." The dancers dance with a shuffling step to suggest the sound of a rasp. How many different sections do you hear in this music? Do you hear any repeated sections? any changing meters?

Quintet No. 2 in C Major

Fourth Movement, "Madrid Retreat"

by Luigi Boccherini

Listen to this music for guitar and string quartet. The composer was describing in music a scene he remembered from Spain. At the signal of a drum, the soldiers would assemble for ceremonies at the close of the day. The music opens quietly with a military theme. The same melody is repeated twelve times and varied each time it is repeated. Follow the numbers as you listen to the variations.

How are dynamic changes achieved?

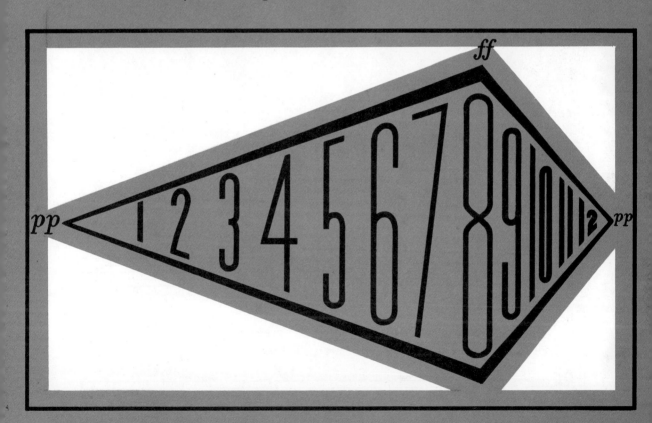

What part of the ceremony do you think the composer is describing?

Na lei o Hawaii

Music by Samuel Kapu
English Words Adapted
from a Text by Mary K. Pukui

1. O fair-est Ha-wai-i, ___ fair le-i is-land, ___
2. O north-ern Kau-a-i, ___ green mo-ki-ha-na, ___
3. A le-i bring to me ___ of sand-y pu-pu, ___

Our gar-land is-land, we wear your red le-hu-a.
Fair mo-ki-ha-na grows high up-on your moun-tains.
The gleam-ing pearl-y shells of Ni-hi-a-u Is-land.

4. Kaulana Oahu your fine ilima,
    Your fine ilima with dainty fragrant blossoms.

5. On isle of Molokai on the candle nut tree,
    Grow silver kukui, leafy silver lei.

6. On little Lanai sweet Kaunaoa
    Sweet Kaunaoa is woven in your garland.

7. For you on Maui are lokelani,
    Are lokelani, red roses for your lei.

8. On peaceful shores, the shores of Kahoolawe,
    On Kahoolawe, come gather hinahina.

9. Ha'ina ia mai ana ka puana,
    Na lei o Hawaii e o mai.

10. Ha'ina hou ia mai ana ka puana,
    Hiiaka ia ka poli a o Pele.

Sacramento

American Sea Chantey
Arranged by Kurt Miller

Many songs rose out of the Gold Rush days in California. Sometimes the songs had new melodies. More often they were melodies people already knew with new words telling of the latest adventures. Stephen Foster's songs, popular at the time, were often used in this way. The melody of this song is a sailor's version of Stephen Foster's "Camptown Races."

1. As   I   was walk- ing on the quay, Hoo - dah, to my hoo - dah,
2. Her hair was brown, her eyes were blue, Hoo - dah, to my hoo - dah,
3. I   raised my   hat and said, "How do?" Hoo - dah, to my hoo - dah.

A   pret - ty   girl   I chanc'd to   see, Hoo - dah, hoo - dah day.
Her lips were red and sweet to   view, Hoo - dah, hoo - dah day.
She bowed and said, "Quite well, thank you." Hoo - dah, hoo - dah day.

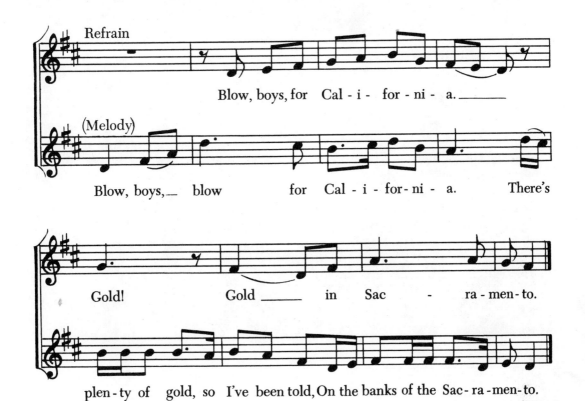

Refrain

Blow, boys, for Cal - i - for - ni - a. _____

(Melody)

Blow, boys,___ blow   for   Cal - i - for - ni - a.   There's

Gold!   Gold _____ in   Sac - ra - men - to.

plen - ty of gold, so I've been told, On the banks of the Sac - ra - men - to.

Old Farmer John

Canadian Folk Song

Learn this song by reading the notes. Begin by discovering the design. Then establish the meter in a moderate tempo, and chant the words in rhythm.

What is the key signature? Find patterns which are made up of tones of the I, V7, and IV chords. Sing the melody on a neutral syllable. Sing it with words.

When you know the song, add an autoharp accompaniment. Find the chords that will harmonize each measure. In some measures you will need two chords.

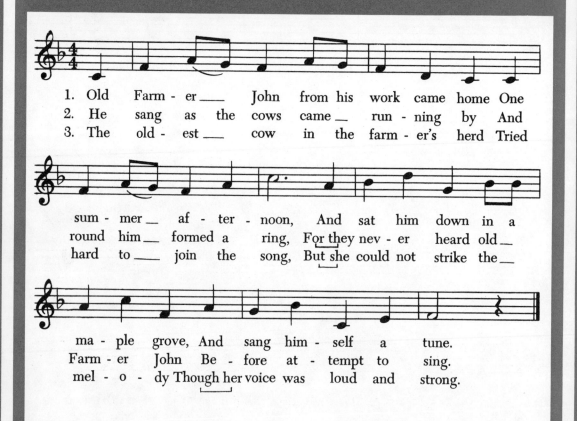

1. Old Farm - er __ John from his work came home One
2. He sang as the cows came __ run - ning by And
3. The old - est __ cow in the farm - er's herd Tried

sum - mer __ af - ter - noon, And sat him down in a
round him __ formed a ring, For they nev - er heard old __
hard to __ join the song, But she could not strike the __

ma - ple grove, And sang him - self a tune.
Farm - er John Be - fore at - tempt to sing.
mel - o - dy Though her voice was loud and strong.

Alaska's Flag

Music by Elinor Dusenburg
Words by Marie Drake

Eight stars of gold on a field of blue, A-
The gold of the ear - ly ___ sour - dough's dreams, The

las - ka's flag, may it mean to you The blue of the sea in the
pre - cious gold of the hills and streams; The bril - liant _ stars in the

1.

eve - ning sky, The moun - tain lakes and the flow'rs near - by;
north - ern sky,

2.

The "Bear," the "Dip-per," and shin-ing high, The great North Star with its

stead - y light, O'er land and sea a bea - con bright, A-

las - ka's flag to A - las-kans dear, The sim- ple flag of a last fron-tier.

Abalone

American Folk Song
Arranged by William S. Haynie

1. In Mon - te - rey   the peo - ple say, "We feed the laz - za - ro - ni
2. Oh, some folks boast of quail on toast be - cause they think it's ton - y,

On car - a - mels and cock - le - shells and hunks of ab - a - lo - ne."
But my tom - cat gets nice and fat   on hunks of ab - a - lo - ne.

Refrain

Ab - a - lo - ne, _____   ab - a - lo - ne, _____

Ab - a - lo - ne, _____   ab - a -

ab - a - lo - ne, _____   And hunks of ab - a -

lo - ne, _____   ab - a - lo - ne,   And hunks of ab - a -

lo - ne,   'ba - lo - ne,   'ba - lo - ne.

lo - ne,   'ba - lo - ne,   'ba - lo - ne.

Night

Music by David Ward-Steinman
Words by William Blake

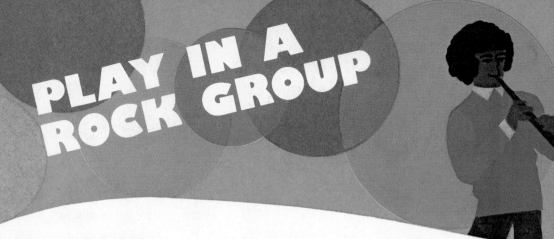

PLAY IN A ROCK GROUP

Begin with the percussion section. The drummer must keep several rhythms going at once. Can you?

1. Begin by tapping the rhythm of the bass drum and sock cymbal. Your right foot is the drum, your left foot hits the pedal for the sock cymbal.

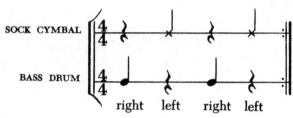

2. Add the rhythm of the suspended cymbal. Use only your right hand. Tap against your knee or thigh.

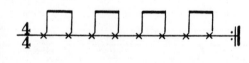

3. Now that you have three things going, add the other hand on the after-beat. Play this rhythm by tapping your left knee or thigh.

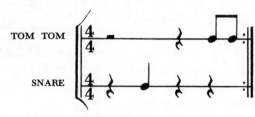

1. Begin with someone playing this pattern on a low instrument:

2. Add a tambourine.

 TAMBOURINE

3. The lead may now improvise around the foundation provided by the rhythm section. Improvise on the xylophone . . .

on any wind instrument . . .

on a keyboard instrument . . .

with your voice.

Use only these pitches: D E F G A.
Change the rhythm as you develop your melody.
Use long sounds or short, quick-moving rhythms—or combine the two.
Repeat melodies exactly or perform them higher or lower.
Have a musical conversation with someone else as you take turns improvising a melody.

More Music to Explore

As you explore more music, make use of all your musical skills. Work as independently as possible.

Follow the steps you have learned for understanding rhythm, melody, and harmony, and read the notation as you sing or play instruments.

Review all you know about design in music. What song forms do you know? What designs have you studied in the listening lessons? Analyze the design of new music you sing or hear.

Review the musical vocabulary you have learned this year. Use the terms as you discuss music.

Review what you know about composing music of your own. Plan compositions for percussion or melody instruments or a combination of instruments.

Attend concerts, and listen to music on radio and television. Discover more music. Build a collection of recordings of music you have studied and other music you like.

Throughout your whole life you can continue to hear, sing, and play music. There always will be something more to study and more music to explore.

Sun Magic

Words and Music
by Donovan Leitch

1. The sun is a ver - y mag - ic fel - low,
2. The wind is a ver - y fick - le fel - low,
3. The rain is a ver - y sad____ la - dy,

He shines down on me each day - ay - ay - ay.____
He blows all my dreams a - way - ay - ay - ay.____
She falls down on me some - times - ime - ime - imes.____

The sun is a ver - y mag - ic fel - low,
The wind is a ver - y fick - le fel - low,
The rain is a ver - y sad____ la - dy,

He shines down on me all day____ ay - ay - ay,____
Blow - in' all my dreams a - way____ ay - ay - ay,____
She falls down on me some - times____ ime - i - imes,____

He shines down on me each day.____
Blow - in' all my dreams a - way.____
She falls down on me some - times.____

172

4. The sea is a very, very old man,
   Deeper than the deepest blue,
   The sea is a very, very old man,
   Deeper than the deepest blue,
   Deeper than the deepest blue.

5. The moon is a typical lady,
   I watch her wax and wane,
   The moon is a typical lady,
   I watch her wax and wane,
   I watch her wax and wane.

6. A star is so very far away, love,
   Just between you and me,
   A star is so very far away, love,
   Just between you and me,
   Just between you and me.

Yankee Doodle Boy

Words and Music
by George M. Cohan

I'm a Yan - kee Doo - dle Dan - dy,

A Yan - kee Doo - dle, do or die;____

A real live neph - ew of my Un - cle Sam,

Born on the Fourth of Ju - ly.____

174

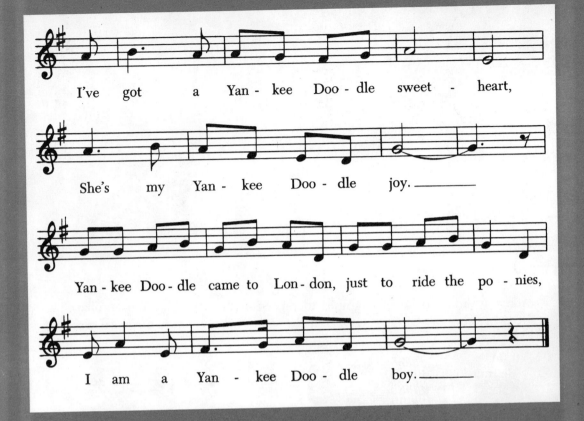

I've got a Yan - kee Doo - dle sweet - heart,

She's my Yan - kee Doo - dle joy. _____

Yan - kee Doo - dle came to Lon - don, just to ride the po - nies,

I am a Yan - kee Doo - dle boy. _____

Symphony No. 3 for Band

Fourth Movement

by Vittorio Giannini

Listen to this music for band written by an American composer of today. Compare it with the march by Sousa discussed on page 7. What differences do you notice? Are there any similarities?

This movement of *Symphony No. 3 for Band* has the same design as the first movement of the *Classical Symphony*, page 134.

Listen to the movement of the symphony for band. Locate the three large sections. How many themes do you hear in section one? How are these themes used in section two? What clue helps you know that the third section is beginning?

Skye Boat Song

Scottish Folk Song

Add the drone sound of bagpipes to this Scottish song. Play the autoharp by depressing the **Gm** and **G** bars at the same time. Strum in a special way.

Refrain

Strum only the low strings.

Verse

Pluck G
Strum

Strum all strings from low to high, then pluck the highest "G" string.

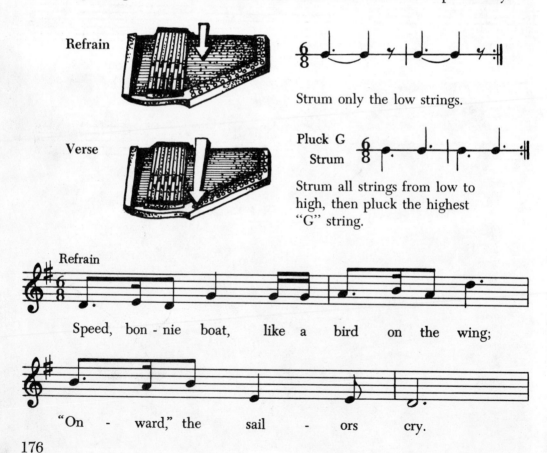

Refrain

Speed, bon - nie boat, like a bird on the wing;

"On - ward," the sail - ors cry.

Car - ry the lad that's born to be king,

Fine

O - ver the sea to Skye.

Verse

1. Loud the winds howl, loud the waves roar,
2. Tho' the waves leap, soft shall ye sleep,

Thun - der - clouds rend the air; Baf - fled, our foes
O - cean's a roy - al bed. Rock'd in the deep,

D.C. al Fine

stand by the shore; Fol - low they will not dare.
Flo - ra will keep Watch by your wea - ry head.

3. Many's the lad fought on that day,
   Well the claymore could wield.
   When the night came, silently lay
   Dead on Culloden's Field.

4. Burn'd are our homes, exile and death
   Scatter the loyal men;
   Yet ere the sword cool in the sheath.
   Charlie will come again.

Seagulls

Music by Richard D. Seidel
Words by Patricia Heyndricks Widmayer

1. I like to watch sea - gulls; they soar and they fly. __
2. I like to watch sea - gulls; they fly high and free. __

They dive in the o - cean and skim through the sky. __
They land on the sand and are bold as can be. __

White wings with black tips and sharp, bead - y black eyes,
They meet in a group on a friend - ly sand - bar,

They scold and they chat - ter and make mourn - ful cries.
Then flap their strong wings and fly off ver - y far.

Surrey Apple-Howler's Song

A Round by Virgil Thomson
Traditional Words

When you know the melody well, sing this song as a round.

1. Here stands ___ a good ap - ple tree. ___

2. Stand fast at root, Bear well at top;

3. Ev - ery lit - tle twig Bear an ap - ple big;

4. Ev - ery lit - tle bough Bear an ap - ple now;

5. Hats full! Caps full! Three score sacks full!

6. Hul - lo, boys! Hul - lo! Hul - lo, boys! Hul - lo!

Little Gypsy Song

Zigeunerliedchen

Music by Robert Schumann
English Words by Kurt Stone

Ev - ery morn - ing, bright and ear - ly,
Je - den Mor - gen, in der Frü - he,

when the day - light makes me rise,
wenn mich weckt das Ta - ges - licht,

I __ feel sad, 'cause I've __ been dream - ing;
mit __ dem Was - ser mei - ner Au - gen

bit - ter tears flow from my eyes.
wasch __ ich dann mein An - ge - sicht.

In my dream I saw the moun - tains
Wo die Ber - ge hoch sich tür - men

in the dis - tance, tow - 'ring high,
an dem Saum des Him - mels dort,

Saw__ a house,__ a love - ly gar - den.
aus __ dem Haus, __ dem schö - nen Gar - ten

D.C. al Fine

I __ was born there; there I'll die.
tra - gen sie bei Nacht mich fort.

Hey, Ho! Anybody Home?

English Round

E minor

Strum an E minor chord as an accompaniment throughout the song.

1.
Hey, ho! An - y - bod - y home?

2.
Meat and drink and mon - ey have I none;

3.
Still I will be ver - y mer - ry!__

Till Eulenspiegel's Merry Pranks

by Richard Strauss

Till Eulenspiegel was a scamp who supposedly lived in Germany during the thirteenth century. He wandered about the country getting in and out of all kinds of mischief. In this composition the composer Strauss describes some of Till's adventures in music. What is such descriptive music called?

The hero, Till Eulenspiegel, has two main themes. The first is quiet and lyric; the other is vigorous and rhythmic. Perhaps they suggest the two sides of Till's character. Listen to each theme carefully until you can recognize it each time it is played. Notice that sometimes the themes are altered as Till goes from one prank to another.

Theme One

Theme Two

The music is divided into ten episodes. The titles will help you imagine what happens in each section. As you listen, notice how the composer has used melody, rhythm, harmony, tone quality, tempo, and dynamics to tell the story.

1. "Once Upon a Time"
2. "Till in the Market Place"
3. "Hidden in a Mouse-Hole"
4. "Disguised as a Monk"
5. "Till Courting Pretty Girls"
6. "The Philistines"
7. "Till's Street Tune"
8. "March"
9. "The Court of Justice"
10. "Finale"

Rock of Ages

Traditional Hebrew Melody
Words by
Frances Fox Sandmel *et. al.*

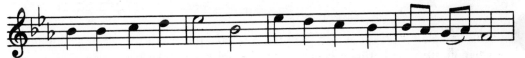

1. Rock of A - ges, God a - bove, Hear we pray our grate-ful song.
2. Kin-dling now the can - dles bright, Greet with joy each glow-ing flame.

Not our pow - er, but thy love And thy spir - it make us strong.
Ded - i - cate your life to right, Faith and free-dom to pro-claim.

Foes have cruel-ly fought us, But thy word has ev-er taught_us
That men may be hear - ing: Lo, the time is near - ing

How to live; Thanks we give, Cour-age thou hast brought_ us.
Which will see All men free, Ty - rants dis - ap - pear - ing.

Take Time in Life

African Dance Song

Enjoy this song from Liberia. Compare it to "Go Down the Wishin' Road" on page 16 and to "Follow the Drinkin' Gourd" on page 84. Do you find any similarities? Why might you expect to?

Clap this rhythm or play it on a small drum as you sing.

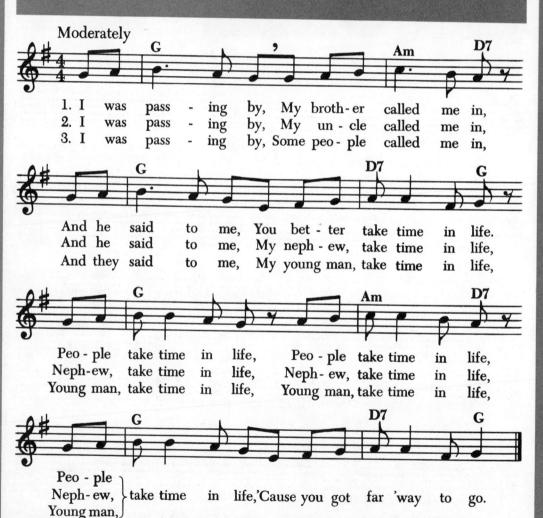

Far from Home

Japanese Folk Song
English Words Adapted

The words of this song tell of a homesick child who has been working away from home in a rice shop. He wishes he were with his parents. The same feelings must have been known by the many Japanese who came thousands of miles to settle along the west coast of the United States.

As the eve-ning falls up-on us,__ A-gain my thoughts turn.__ They turn back to my__ home,__ The place I long__ to re-turn__ to a-gain, The place I long to be. I spend the long days__ work-ing, And when the eve-ning falls I long__ to go back to my home.

eve-ning falls I long__ to go back to my home.

Leron, Leron

Philippine Folk Melody
Words by Beth Landis

1. Le - ron, Le - ron, my dear, Le - ron, Le - ron, come here!
2. Le - ron, Le - ron, my dear, Le - ron, Le - ron, come here!

That bruise up - on your knee Is all for love of me.
That bruise up - on your head, Re - mem - ber what I said?

Those ripe pa - pa - yas sweet up - on the branch - es high
Your bas - ket fill with fruit less lus - cious than you wish;

Your bas - ket may not fill, for them you must not try.
To me it tastes as sweet as an - y in the dish.

Study the rhythm of the song. How many different motives do you find?

This song is in two-part harmony. Can you name the different intervals that are included?

Tinikling

Philippine Folk Dance

In which of our states might songs and dances from the Philippines be best known?

This Philippine dance gets its name from a bird, "Tikling," that looks like a crane or heron. The dance imitates the way the bird walks in tall grass and over branches on the ground in the forest.

Two players sit on the floor opposite each other, holding the ends of bamboo poles which rest on pieces of wood. They slide the poles and click them together on count one of the music. They lift the poles a foot apart and tap them on the pieces of wood for counts two and three. That rhythm—click, tap, tap—continues throughout the dance.

Two dancers face each other beside the poles. They leap sideways into and out of the space between the poles, first on the right foot, then on the left, as the poles come together and move apart.

Listen to the traditional music for "Tinikling." Discover the meter and the design of the melody. Practice the rhythm with the bamboo poles. Practice the dance steps with chalk lines or with the poles at rest on the floor. When you know the steps, do the traditional dance. Later improvise some new steps of your own.

You have played the autoharp many times by placing the instrument on a table and strumming an accompaniment. Let's explore another way of holding this instrument.

Do you remember who the troubadours were? They were travelling musicians of long ago who wandered from place to place singing and playing instruments. They usually played plucked string instruments. You can hold the autoharp in a way that will allow you to stroll around freely.

Holding the autoharp

Sit in a chair and pick up the autoharp. Position it like this:

flat side near chin

small section of corner tucked under right arm

curve resting on left arm so that left hand can reach chord buttons on bars.

188

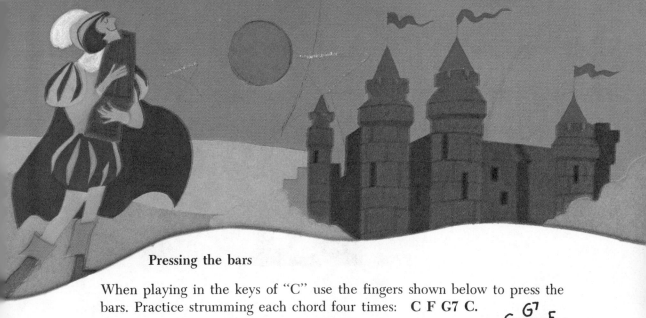

Pressing the bars

When playing in the keys of "C" use the fingers shown below to press the bars. Practice strumming each chord four times: **C F G7 C.**

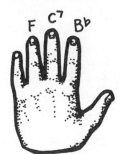

For the key of F, use these fingers. Practice strumming four times:
F B♭ C7 F.

When you feel very secure holding the instrument, walk as you strum. Try changing the direction of your walking each time you change chords. Remember to press bars down firmly to produce a clear sound.

A new stroke

Use only the middle strings. Pick a string at random and pluck it with your thumb. Then quickly brush down, using the fingernails of the other fingers. Brush across the strings within easy reach.

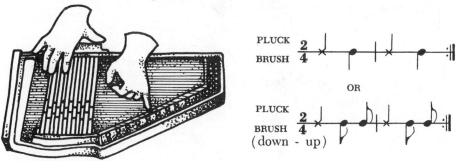

Use this stroke to accompany "Old Joe Clarke," page 76. You will need only the **F** and **C7** chords. Can you walk as you sing and play?

189

Mary Ann

Calypso Song
Words by Kathy Alexander

Notice the syncopated rhythms in this calypso song from the West Indies. Practice chanting the words. Sometimes the accent on a syllable in a word is changed to fit the syncopated rhythm. After you have practiced, listen to the recording to see if you have learned the rhythm correctly.

1. All day, __ all night, __ Miss Mar - y Ann, _____
2. If you __ come to __ this is - land fine, _____

Down by __ the sea - side, __ sift - ing sand; _____
You'll love __ the sea and __ bright sun - shine, _____

All the lit - tle chil - dren __ love Mar - y Ann, _____
You will be __ en - chant - ed __ with this fair land, _____

You, too, __ will love her, __ Miss Mar - y Ann. _____
You'll be __ be - witched by __ Miss Mar - y Ann. _____

Compose Your Own
Percussion Accompaniment

The interesting cross rhythms created by the percussion patterns are one of the unique features of calypso. Rhythms to accompany a calypso song or dance are built upward like layers of a cake. Follow this plan and build your own accompaniment for "Mary Ann."

Practice these patterns separately. Then combine them until you can play them easily and can hear the intertwined rhythms.

The Musician at Work... in a Radio Station

If you were a musician working in a radio station you might be a:

DISC JOCKEY

You would need to:

- know current recordings.

- know the history of popular music.

- be aware of the current "pop scene."

- select appealing recordings for each broadcast.

- know interesting biographical information about recording artists.

CONCERT HOUR COMMENTATOR

You would need to:

- select an interesting variety of music for each broadcast.

- know about performers, composers, and many styles of music.

- be able to pronounce composers' names, musical terms, instruments, and titles of musical compositions.

- be very familiar with a wide variety of recordings.

BROADCAST ENGINEER

You would need to:

- be able to operate electronic equipment.

- hear specific places in music appropriate for fading in and out.

- be able to determine the proper sound level for various types of music.

STATION LIBRARIAN

You would need to:

- maintain, catalog, and locate tapes, records, and sound effects needed for each broadcast.

DEVELOP A RADIO STATION AT YOUR SCHOOL

1. Choose jobs—be sure you can become qualified for the job.
2. Plan and perform radio broadcasts.
3. Tape-record your program.
4. Make arrangements to broadcast the tape over the school public address system.

WRITER-RESEARCHER

You would need to:

- be able to locate facts about the date and place a work was first performed.

- research biographical data on composers and performers.

- write scripts and commentaries for interviewers and disc jockeys.

- make suggestions about program content and format.

Pupu O Ewa

(Shells of Ewa)

Hawaiian Folk Song

It is believed that this song was written for the dedication of a chapel on Oahu, one of the islands in the Hawaiian chain. The words mean:

> Beautiful Kaala, flawless in the calm,
> Famous mountain of Ewa;
> It brings the wind of the land.
> The Moae (trade wind) replies, "Here I am, beloved."
> Seashells of Ewa, a multitude of people;
> Come all and see this new thing in the land,
> A land that is famous from the days of our ancestors.
> Everywhere in Pu'uloa is the trail of Kaahupahau.

¡Qué bonita bandera!

Beautiful Is Our Banner

Puerto Rican Folk Song
Words Adapted

All people have songs which tell of their pride in their homeland. This patriotic song is sung by the people of Puerto Rico.

194

Land of My Fathers

Music by John James
Words by Beth Landis

The music for this song is by a Welsh composer who lived in the early 1800's. The words in your book were written recently by an American. Although the melody is Welsh, the pride of country expressed in the words could be the thoughts of people of many lands.

1. O land of my fa - thers, O land dear to __ me,
2. O land of my fa - thers, O land dear to __ me,

A land of brave men and fine wom - en is she;
A land of the po - ets and sing - ers is she;

Her __ lov - ers of __ free - dom, Her __ he - roes of __ old
Her __ words ring in the air, ___ Her __ harp sounds ev - ery - where;

Have called this great coun - try their home. _____
I call this great coun - try my home. _____

Refrain

Great Land! Land of green val - leys and hills;

As __ strong as the sea, as __ fair and as free;

I call this great coun - try my home. _____

Round for Umbrella & Percussion

Write and perform a round for percussion. Create rhythm patterns with long and short sounds and moments of silence. First, determine a meter for the round. Then, write the rhythm patterns on a strip of paper. Mark a beginning signal on the notation. Attach the paper around the bottom of an umbrella.

Choose a person to play the basic beat on a drum. A leader stands in the middle and slowly turns the umbrella. The performers place themselves in four areas around the umbrella. Each enters when the beginning signal passes him. He plays the rhythm patterns as they appear.

The Star-Spangled Banner

Composer Unknown
Words by Francis Scott Key

1. Oh, __ say, can you see   by the dawn's ear - ly   light,
2. On the shore, dim - ly   seen   thro' the mists of   the   deep,
3. Oh, __ thus be   it   ev-er   when __ free   men   shall stand

What so proud - ly we   hailed   at the twi - light's last gleam-ing?
Where the foe's haugh-ty   host   in dread si - lence re - pos - es,
Be - tween their loved homes and the war's des - o - la - tion!

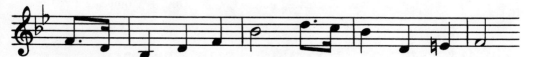

Whose broad stripes and bright stars, through the per - il - ous fight,
What is   that which the breeze, o'er the tow - er - ing   steep,
Blest with vic - t'ry and peace, may the heav'n-res - cued land

O'er the ram - parts we watched were so gal - lant - ly stream-ing?
As it fit - ful - ly   blows, half con - ceals, half dis - clos - es?
Praise the Pow'r that hath made and pre-served us   a   na - tion.

And the rock - ets' red glare, the bombs burst - ing in   air,
Now it catch - es the gleam of the morn - ing's first beam,
Then __ con - quer we must, for our cause it   is   just,

Gave proof through the night that our flag was still there.
In full glo - ry re - flec-ted now ___ shines on the stream;
And this be our mot-to: "In ___ God is our trust."

Oh, say, does that ___ star - span - gled ban - ner ___ yet ___ wave ___
'Tis the star - span - gled ___ ban - ner, Oh, long may ___ it ___ wave ___
And the star - span - gled ___ ban - ner in tri - umph ___ shall ___ wave ___

O'er the land ___ of the free and the home of the brave?
O'er the land ___ of the free and the home of the brave!
O'er the land ___ of the free and the home of the brave!

Music for Special Times

Now Thank We All Our God

Melody by Johann Crüger
Words by Martin Rinckart
Translation by Catherine Winkworth

Listen to the recording of this well-known chorale. First you hear children sing it with an organ accompaniment written by Felix Mendelssohn. Then you hear Johann Sebastian Bach's arrangement which has been recorded with choir, two trumpets, and organ. The trumpets play interludes between the phrases which the choir sings.

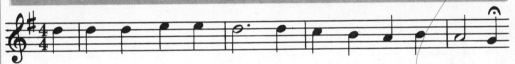

1. Now thank we all our God With heart and hands and voic - es,
2. O may this boun - teous God Through all our life be near us,

Who won - drous things hath done, In whom his world re - joic - es,
With ev - er joy - ful hearts And bless - ed peace to cheer us,

Who, from our moth - ers' arms, Hath blessed us on our way
And keep us in his grace, And guide us when per - plexed,

With count - less gifts of love, And still is ours to - day.
And free us from all ills In this world and the next.

Thanksgiving Canon

Traditional Canon

For Thy gra - cious bless - ings, For Thy won - drous

For Thy gra - cious bless - ings,

word, For Thy lov - ing kind - ness

For Thy won - drous word, For Thy lov - ing

We give thanks, Oh, Lord.

kind - ness We give thanks, Oh, Lord.

O Hanukah

Yiddish Folk Song
Translated by Judith Eisenstein

O Ha - nu - kah, O Ha - nu - kah, come light the me - no - rah,

Let's have a par - ty, we'll all dance the ho - ra.

Gath - er round the ta - ble, we'll give you a treat,

Shin - ing tops to play with and pan - cakes to eat;

And while we are play - ing the can - dles are burn - ing — low.

One for each night, they — shed a sweet light To re -

mind us of days long a - go. mind us of days long a - go.

Here We Come A-Wassailing

Old English Carol

1. Here we come a - was - sail - ing A - mong the leaves so green; __
2. We are not dai - ly beg - gars That beg from door to door; __
3. Good mas - ter and mis - tress, As you sit by the fire, __
4. God bless the mas - ter of this house, Like-wise the mis - tress, too, __

Here we come a - wan - d'ring, So fair ___ to be seen.
But we are neigh - bors' chil - dren Whom you have seen be - fore.
Pray think of us poor chil - dren Who wan - der in the mire.
And all the lit - tle chil - dren That round the ta - ble go.

Refrain

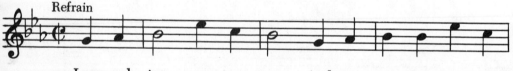

Love and joy come to you, And to you glad Christ-mas

too; And God bless you and send __ you a hap - py New

Year, And God send you a hap - py New __ Year. __

Joy to the World

Attributed to George Frideric Handel
Arranged by Lowell Mason
Words by Isaac Watts

1. Joy to the world! the Lord is come: Let earth re - ceive her King;
2. Joy to the earth! the Sav - ior reigns: Let men their songs em - ploy;
3. He rules the world with truth and grace, And makes the na - tions prove

Let ev - ery __ heart __ pre - pare __ him __ room, __
While fields __ and __ floods, __ rocks, hills, __ and __ plains __
The glo - ries __ of __ his right - eous - ness, __

And heav'n and na - ture __ sing, and __ heav'n and na - ture __ sing,
Re - peat the sound - ing __ joy, re - peat the sound - ing __ joy,
And won - ders of his __ love, and __ won - ders of his __ love,

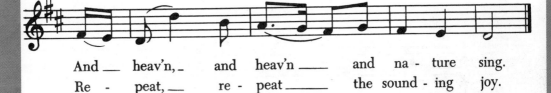

And __ heav'n, __ and heav'n __ and na - ture sing.
Re - peat, __ re - peat __ the sound - ing joy.
And __ won - ders, won - ders of his love.

March of the Kings

French Folk Melody
Translated by Satis Coleman

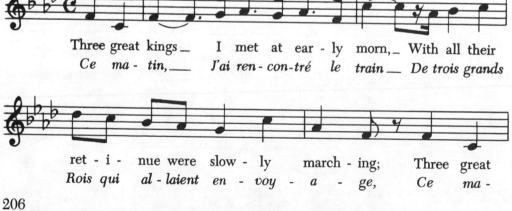

Three great kings _ I met at ear - ly morn, _ With all their
Ce ma - tin, _ J'ai ren - con - tré le train _ De trois grands

ret - i - nue were slow - ly march - ing; Three great
Rois qui al - laient en - voy - a - ge, Ce ma -

kings ___ I met at ear - ly morn, ___ Were on their
tin, ___ J'ai ren - con - tré le train ___ De trois grands

way to meet the new - ly born. With gifts of
Rois des - sus le grand che - min. Tout char - gés

gold brought from far a - way, ___ And val - iant
d'or les sui - vaient d'a - bord ___ De grands guer -

war - riors to guard the king - ly treas - ure, With gifts of
riers et les gar - des du tré - sor, ___ Tout char - gés

gold brought from far a - way, ___ And shields all
d'or les sui - vaient d'a - bord ___ De grands guer -

shin - ing in their bright ar - ray.
riers a - vec leurs bou - cli - ers.

How Far to Bethlehem?

Music by Mary E. Caldwell
Words Adapted from G. K. Chesterton by Mary E. Caldwell

1. How far to Beth-le-hem? Not ver-y far.

Shall we find the sta-ble-room lit by a star?

Can we see the lit-tle Child; is he with-in?

If we lift the wood-en latch, may we go in?

(Melody) Brighter

2. May we stroke the creat-ures there, ox-en and sheep?
May we watch like them and see Je-sus a-sleep?

Brighter

May we stroke them, ox-en and sheep?
May we watch Je-sus a-sleep?

If we touch his ti-ny hand, will he a-wake?

Will he know we've come so far ___ just for ___ his sake?

3. Great ___ kings have pre - cious gifts, but we have naught;

Lit - tle smiles and lit - tle tears are all we've brought.

Ah, ___ chil - dren, Mar - y must weep,

For all wea - ry lit - tle chil - dren Mar - y must weep.

Ah, ___ chil - dren, sleep, chil - dren, sleep.

Here up - on his bed of straw, ___ O sleep, chil - dren, sleep.

And the Trees Do Moan

Southern Mountain Folk Song

1. In the val - ley_ of Ju - de - a, Cold and win - try_ blown,
2. Mar - y took her_ lit - tle ba - by, Set out all a - lone;

Christ was born one_ frost - y morn - ing, And the trees do_ moan.
Down in E - gypt_ land they tar - ried, Where the trees do_ moan.

Dark - en'd skies, and men a - stum - bling; High a - bove there shone
Je - sus then be - came a car-pen-ter, Work'd with wood and stone;

One bright star a - mov - ing East - ward, Where the trees do moan.
Nails he drove and cross - arms fash - ion'd, And the trees do moan.

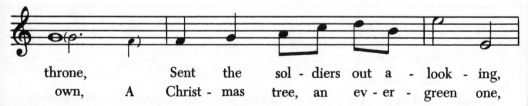

Her - od and the rul - ing Ro - mans State - ly sat up - on the
There one day while in the for - est black, One tree he pick'd for his

throne, Sent the sol - diers out a - look - ing,
own, A Christ - mas tree, an ev - er - green one,

210

And the trees do moan, And the trees do moan.
And the trees do moan, And the trees do moan.

In the Bleak Mid-Winter

Music by Gustav Holst
Words by Christina Rossetti

1. In the bleak mid - win - ter, Frost - y wind made moan,
2. What __ can I give Him, Poor __ as I am?

Earth stood hard as i - ron, Wa - ter like a stone;
If I were a shep - herd, I would bring a lamb;

Snow had fall - en, snow on snow, Snow __ on __ snow,
If I were a wise __ man, I would do my part; Yet

In the bleak mid - win - ter, Long _____ a - go.
what I can I give Him— Give _____ my heart.

211

See the Many Lights

Miren cuantas luces

Spanish Folk Song
English Words by Elena Paz

1. See the man - y lights, How they glit - ter __ bright - ly
1. ¡Mi - ren cuán - tas lu - ces, cuán - tos res - plan - do - res!
2. Three __ kings so wise Has - ten to the __ man - ger

O - ver Beth - le - hem.
Sin du - da es Be - lén.
Bear - ing gifts so rare,

O shep - herds, what glo - ry!
¡Qué glo - ria, pas - to - res!
And bas - kets of flow - ers,

O shep - herds, what glo - ry!
¡Qué glo - ria, pas - to - res!
And bas - kets of flow - ers.

212

The Pilgrims

Los peregrinos

Spanish Folk Song
English Words by Elena Paz

Wearily

(The pilgrims) 1. From dis - tant lands so wea - ry,
(Los peregrinos) *1. De lar - ga jor - na - da*
(The Innkeepers) 2. Who, on this night so drear - y,

We've come up - on your door, ___
ren - di - dos lle - ga - mos,
Our com - fort dares dis - turb? ___

Night has ___ fall - en drear - y!
y a - sí lo im - plo - ra - mos
Here, by our blaze so cheer - y,

Wel - come us, we im - plore. ___
pa - ra des - can - sar. ___
Your pleas must go un - heard. ___

213

La Piñata

Spanish Folk Song

Alla marcia

1. En las no - ches de po - sa - da, la pi -
2. Con tus o - ji - tos ven - da - dos y en las

ña - ta es lo me - jor;_____ Aun las ni - ñas re - mil
ma - nos un Bas - tón,_____ ¡la o-lla róm - pe - la a pe -

ga - das se a - ni - man con gran fer - vor:
da - zos! ¡No le ten - gas com - pa - sión!

Allegretto

Da - le da - le da - le, No pier - das el ti - no
Que si no le das ____ ¡de un pa - lo te e - pi - no!

mi - de la dis - tan - cia que hay en el ca - mi - no.
¡Por - que tie - nes au - ra, de pu - ro pe - pi - no!

214

In Mexico and some sections of the United States, the *Posadas* is celebrated for nine nights. Each evening the children of the village process through the village, singing special songs. Each child carries a candle.

As they wind their way through the streets, they knock on doors, asking for shelter, as did Joseph and Mary the night Jesus was born. Finally, one house bids the pilgrims enter. Inside is a **nacimiento** or manger. After more songs and prayers, refreshments are served.

Then it is time to break the **piñata**, a large container in the form of an animal or bird. Inside the brightly decorated container are toys, coins, fruits, nuts, and candies. The *piñata* is hung by a rope from the ceiling. Starting with the youngest child present, each is blindfolded, turned around three times and given a stick with which he tries to break the *piñata*. Each child gets a turn until one finally succeeds in breaking it. Then everyone scrambles for the goodies which have fallen on the floor.

Learn the songs on pages 212-214 which are part of the Mexican celebration, *Las Posadas*. Then plan your own procession and dramatization. Perhaps you can make a *piñata* from papier-mâché. You could include the *piñata* game in your play.

God Bless America

Words and Music
by Irving Berlin

Let's Explore Art

Home Ranch, detail, 1888,
Thomas Eakins (1844-1916,
United States). Oil, 24″ x 20″.
Collection of the Philadelphia
Museum of Art.

Spring, 1914, Joseph Stella (1880-1946, Italy, United States).
Oil on canvas, 75″ x 40⅛″.
Yale University Art Gallery. Gift of Collection Société Anonyme.

Let's Explore Art

The works of art included in this book represent all regions of the United States. Some were created during early times; others are very recent. Some reflect art of other countries and some are very American. As you study the examples, try to decide when each artist lived. In what section of the country did each artist have a special interest? Can you find clues in his subject, materials, and style?

You have studied folk music and music created by composers. In this section of your book you will find some works of art created by folk artists. Other works were created by individuals who devoted their lives to art. You can enjoy art by creating works of your own and by observing works of others. Works of art often are purchased by individuals to enjoy in their homes, or by public museums to be enjoyed by everyone. You might like to collect works of art. If there is a museum in your community, take a class trip to visit it. Ask to see the works by American artists.

Look at the works of art throughout your book. Discuss the subject of each work. What does the artist suggest that would not be in a photograph? How does his choice of material and method of working convey his ideas?

Dad's Coming, Winslow Homer (1836-1910, United States). Engraving. Harper's Weekly, November 1, 1873.

Ship's Figurehead, c. 1830. Wood.
Courtesy, Shelburne Museum,
Shelburne, Vermont.

In what section of the country would you expect artists to use the sea as a subject? Review the sea songs you have learned.

Ralph Wheelock's Farm, 1822, Francis Alexander (1800-1880, United States). Oil on canvas, 27" x 48⅛".
National Gallery of Art, Washington, D.C. Gift of Edgar William and
Bernice Chrysler Garbisch.

The two artists whose works are represented on this page lived at about the same time, but in different states. Can you decide where they might have lived?

Penn's Treaty with the Indians, 1840, Edward Hicks (1780-1849, United States). Oil on canvas, 24¼" x 30⅛".
Collection of Edgar William and Bernice Chrysler Garbisch.

Street Shadows, Jacob Lawrence (1917-   , United States). Tempera on gesso, 23¾" x 29½".
Collection of Mr. and Mrs. Lewis J. Garlick, New York.

In these paintings you see two artists' responses to the same city. Discuss the differences in their ideas and in their materials and methods of painting.

Lower Manhattan (Composing derived from top of Woolworth), 1922, John Marin (1870-1953, United States). Watercolor, 21⅝" x 26⅞".
Collection: The Museum of Modern Art, New York. Acquired through the Lillie P. Bliss Bequest, 1945.

Geodesic Bubble, The United States Pavillion, Montreal Expo '67, R. Buckminster Fuller, architect (1895- , United States).

Russ Kinne from Photo Researchers

Old Meeting House, 1816, Lancaster, Mass., Charles Bulfinch, architect (1763-1844, United States). Brick and wood.

Many buildings in our country have styles of architecture that come from other countries. We have also developed some styles that are very American, such as those shown on this page. Visit public buildings and churches in your community. Discuss whether they are truly American or have been influenced by styles from Europe, Latin America, or the Orient.

Lever House, 1952, New York City, Skidmore, Owings & Merrill, architects. Steel-frame and glass building.

The art works on this page and "Street Shadows" on page 222 were created by Black American artists. The art of our country, as well as the music, has been enriched by the contributions of people who came to America from many different lands.

Chester, Sargent Johnson (1888- , United States). Terra cotta, 8½″ x 5½″ x 6″.
San Francisco Museum of Art. Albert M. Bender Collection.

Folksinger, Hartwell Yeargans. Lithograph from *Prints by American Negro Artists,* T. V. Roelof-Lanner, Editor, 1967.
Courtesy, Cultural Exchange Center Publishers, Los Angeles, California.

Home on the Mississippi River,
artist unknown (about 1865).
Oil on canvas, 16⅛″ x 24¼″.
Collection of Edgar William
and Bernice Chrysler Garbisch.

Handwork, such as embroidery, applique, whittling, and carving, has always been popular in the United States. Do any of your adult friends or relatives enjoy doing such handwork? Bring examples to class.

Quilt, applique, made in Virginia in 1853.
National Gallery of Art, Washington, D.C. Index of American Design.

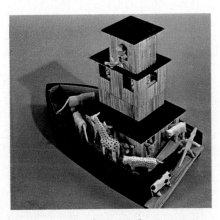

Noah's Ark with Animals, Campton, Kentucky, 1969, Edgar Tolson (1905?- , United States). Animals whittled from wood with penknife, ark built of ice cream sticks.
Collection of Michael D. Hall, Lexington, Kentucky.

Dinner for Threshers (detail), 1933, two studies for right and left sections of the painting, Grant Wood (1892-1942, United States). Pencil, 17¾″ x 26¾″.
Collection: Whitney Museum of American Art, New York.

226

In these paintings of the Midwest, what common subjects have the artists presented? In what ways do their styles differ?

My Egypt, 1927, Charles Demuth (1883-1935, United States). Oil on composition board, 35¾″ x 30″.
Collection: Whitney Museum of American Art, New York.

Important events in our history and heroes who have helped to build our country are remembered in many ways. Sometimes we remember them by erecting monuments in public places. Some class members may have seen the two monuments shown on this page. In your community, is there a monument to an important event or a famous person? If so, visit it and learn why and when it was built and who designed it.

Thomas Jefferson Memorial, Washington, D.C. dedicated 1943, John Russell Pope, architect.

Dept. of Interior National Park Service Photo by M. Woodbridge Williams

Jefferson National Expansion Memorial Arch, St. Louis, Missouri, 1967, Eero Saarinen (1910-1961, Finland, United States). Stainless steel, 630′.

Hans Namuth from Photo Researchers

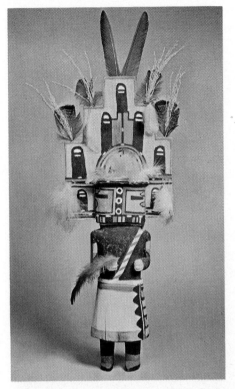

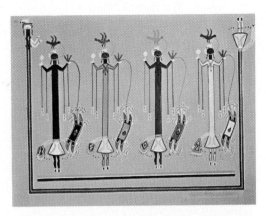

Big Godway Ceremony. Sand painting.
Museum of Navaho Ceremonial Art,
Santa Fe, New Mexico.

Painted Kachina doll representing Humis Kachina, 25″ high, Hopi Indians, Arizona.
Heye Foundation, Museum of the
American Indian, New York.

The folk art on this page is from the Far West. Can you use some of the materials the Indians used to create art of your own?

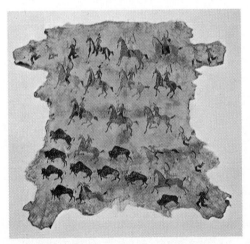

Painted elkskin robe representing a buffalo hunt. 63″ x 50″, Crow Indians, Montana.
Heye Foundation, Museum of the
American Indian, New York.

Silver squash blossom necklace with "naja." Pendant, 12½″ long, Navajo, New Mexico.
Heye Foundation, Museum of the
American Indian, New York.

Merced River, Yosemite Valley, Albert Bierstadt (1830-1902, United States). Oil on canvas, 36″ x 50″.

The Metropolitan Museum of Art, New York. Gift of the sons of William Paton, 1909.

Look at the nineteenth century painting on this page. Look at the three paintings by Contemporary American artists on page 231 and page 218. What feeling and meaning does each suggest to you? What in the painting causes your response? Discuss the method of painting used by each artist. Create paintings of your own using one or more of these methods.

Broadcast, 1959, Robert Rauschenberg (1925-   , United States).
Combine painting, 5'2" x 6'4". Private collection, Milan.

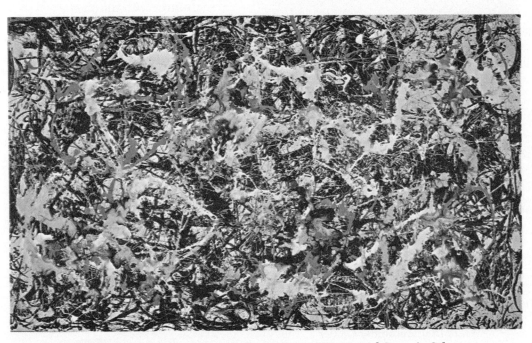

Convergence, 1952, Jackson Pollock (1912-1956, United States). Oil on
canvas, 93½" x 155".
Albright-Knox Art Gallery, Buffalo, New York. Gift of Seymour H. Knox.

The Bronco Buster, 1890's,
Frederic Remington (1861-1909,
United States). Statuette group,
bronze, height—23″, length—15″.
The Metropolitan Museum of Art,
New York. Rogers Fund, 1907.

Compare the two Contemporary
sculptures with the one by
Remington, who lived in the
nineteenth century. How do the
ideas, materials, and
methods differ?

Fountains, Len Lye (1901-   ,
United States). Motorized kinetic
steel sculpture.
Courtesy, Howard Wise Gallery.

White Lily, Alexander Calder
(1898-   , United States). Sheet
metal and wire, height—41¾″.
City Art Museum of St. Louis.

Classified Index

Rounds and Canons

Alphabetical Index of Music and Poetry